Praise for
Success in Africa
and **Jonathan Berman**

"We are beginning to see Africa's moment in the sun—it has been home to some of the world's fastest growing economies over the last two decades, while extreme poverty rates have sharply declined and key health indicators have improved. In *Success in Africa,* some of today's most influential business leaders share their firsthand insights about working on a continent bright with shared opportunity, and explain why Africa's future is more promising than ever."

—**President Bill Clinton**

"Africa is bigger, faster growing, more profitable, and significantly more important than you'd like to admit. If you've been overlooking a $2 trillion economy, it's time to start paying attention."

—**Seth Godin**, best-selling author of
Linchpin, Tribes, The Dip, and others

"Jonathan Berman beautifully puts the lurid popular press headlines about Africa into perspective and helps us peek behind that curtain of stereotypes with insights regarding how investors can prosper in Africa. His extensive experience on a wide range of Africa projects is dynamite. I particularly loved his human insights—the energetic resourceful ambitious Africans surmounting the enormous barriers of poor infrastructure and inefficient governments. Altogether, it's a very important book."

—**Mark Mobius**, executive chairman,
Templeton Emerging Markets

"*Success in Africa* is an admirable piece of cross-cutting analysis, delivering a new understanding of Africa from the viewpoint of global business leaders and the new class of rising African businessmen. Jonathan Berman brings both networks to bear on the question of what drives success in Africa, and indeed in fast-growth markets worldwide. While explaining the very significant challenges of business in Africa, he also highlights how some in Africa are defining a new path to growth, one that improves on the mistakes of the past (including those of the West)."

—**Paul Collier**, Oxford University professor, best-selling author of *The Bottom Billion*

"This is a not-to-be-missed primer on not only where Africa has come from but how the future is unfolding. It will help change the skeptic's view of Africa. Great book."

—**Neville Isdell**, former CEO, The Coca Cola Company

SUCCESS
IN AFRICA

SUCCESS IN AFRICA

CEO INSIGHTS FROM A CONTINENT ON THE RISE

JONATHAN BERMAN

First published by Bibliomotion, Inc.

33 Manchester Road
Brookline, MA 02446
Tel: 617-934-2427
www.bibliomotion.com

Printed in the United States of America

Library of Congress Cataloging-in-Publication Data

Berman, Jonathan E., author.
    Success in Africa : CEO insights from a continent on the rise / by Jonathan E. Berman.
        page cm
    Includes bibliographical references and index.
    ISBN 978-1-937134-46-4 (hardcover : alk. paper) — ISBN 978-1-937134-47-1 (ebook) — ISBN 978-1-937134-48-8 (enhanced ebook)
    1. Economic development—Africa.   2. Africa—Economic conditions—1960–
3. Africa—Commerce.   I. Title.
    HC800.B457 2013
    338.96—dc23
                                    2013016001

For Monica and Boaz, who inspire

CONTENTS

FOREWORD

by Robert E. Rubin

former co-chairman Goldman Sachs,
U.S. Secretary of the Treasury (1995–1999)

When I've had to assess complex environments, I've often sought insight from people who have navigated those environments effectively. *Success in Africa* delivers those insights.

I recall thinking when I visited Africa as Treasury Secretary fifteen years ago that the problems are immense and obvious, yet there also seem to be enormous opportunities and a lot of situations where the risks may be considerable but the rewards far greater. As I spent time in South Africa, Namibia, Kenya, Mozambique, and the Ivory Coast, I was involved with finance ministers, central bankers, and other government officials, but I also looked through the prism of my business career at the opportunities for the private sector and entrepreneurs. I was intrigued by the potential I saw then.

That promise seems even greater today. Political and other conditions have improved in many countries and the availability of investment capital in Africa continues to lag way behind the opportunity for investment.

Jonathan Berman is among the professionals closing that gap. I first got to know Jonathan through the Council on Foreign Relations, where he's been an active and creative member. In the early months of 2012, we discussed a book he was interested in writing, drawing on the insights of CEOs succeeding in Africa. Africa's changed a great deal since I visited, as has the rest of the world. Today, the world's most mature economies—the United States, Europe, and Japan—are experiencing various degrees of current economic difficulty, and many emerging market economies are facing complexity with respect to the shorter-term outlook. Africa has challenges as well, but is still relatively undiscovered by investors and business.

Among most financial people and business professionals, the understanding of Africa is neither very deep nor very wide. *Success in Africa* does for readers what Jonathan has done in the past for me: introduce a number of the CEOs who have succeeded in Africa, and add his own perspective, to provide greater insight into an increasingly important and too often misunderstood part of the world.

Some of the insights in these pages are from CEOs of storied American companies like General Electric and Coca Cola. They have adapted to compete and win in fast-growth markets including Africa. Then there are the voices of African CEOs, men, and women who have built successful companies from Morocco to South Africa. Reading their views is enlightening because they know what succeeds on their home turf. This reflects my own experience in emerging economies, where the best sources of useful and reliable information are often successful local business people. By local, I do not mean small or provincial. Graham Mackay, who's from Swaziland, built South African Breweries (now SABMiller) into a global beverage company with a $54 billion market capitalization, generating 13 percent of its earnings from emerging Africa. These are globally competitive companies winning in a fast growth market.

Looking at both the American and the African CEOs' experience in Africa, there is much to be learned. GE CEO Jeff Immelt's description of how he manages uncertainty in these markets speaks to the probabilistic thinking that, in my view, best informs business and policy decisions on all issues. The thoughts of James Mwangi (*Forbes'* Africa CEO of the Year) about the journey from tradition to modernity display an understanding of, and deep empathy with, the African banking customer. It's a level of customer insight that contributes greatly to the success of any business operating in new markets.

I remember President Clinton saying on return from his presidential trip to Africa that too often Africa is seen as one entity with serious and perhaps overwhelming problems, instead of a realistic view of Africa as a continent with different regions and nations with distinct political, economic, and social conditions, some quite promising. That realism is as necessary and valuable today as it was then.

In some circles, there is optimism about Africa that may well be running ahead of the facts, just as in other circles, the discussion is still dominated by traditional views of Africa as a single entity beset by intractable problems. Neither of these perspectives serves the interests of those involved in those discussions nor the interests of Africa. *Success in Africa* draws on the views and experiences of business leaders to provide a balanced view of Africa today. And, that makes *Success in Africa* essential reading for all who are interested in Africa for reasons of business, investment, policy, or curiosity.

TABLE OF FIGURES

Table of Figures

CHAPTER 1

Welcome to the Frontier

Mark Zuckerberg in his hoodie. Steve Jobs on stage. Sergey Brin in jeans and Eric Schmidt, not. It would be hard to understand the extraordinary rise of Silicon Valley without understanding a bit about its leaders, their background and ambitions. At the frontier of technology, the social and business paradigms are new. The leaders in that market help us map it, understand it, and access it. We also enjoy reading about them. The men and women who succeed on the frontier are compelling characters through whom we come to understand a new horizon.

It was much the same way when the continental U.S. economy was coming together at the dawn of the twentieth century. The implications for the United States and the world were massive and, for many at the time, difficult to grasp. Characters like John D. Rockefeller, Andrew Carnegie, and J. P. Morgan helped define the times.

If you picked up this book, chances are you're aware of a new horizon in a place many had written off: Africa. You may have heard that six of the ten fastest-growing markets in the world are in Africa; that it is growing as fast as India, and at twice the rate of Brazil; that 60 percent of the world's future farming potential is in Africa. If you follow global markets, you've probably heard a lot about "frontier markets," and that Africa leads this pack. If you own GE stock, you received a 2012 annual report highlighting Africa, where CEO Jeff Immelt anticipates the company may sell more gas turbines than in the U.S. over the next several years.[1]

What drives success in a frontier market like Africa? What are the biggest challenges and how are they overcome? Is it different from other places you've worked? Does it even make sense to speak of "Africa," which, after all, encompasses fifty-four countries?

Few businesspeople know frontier markets like Africa well or what it takes to succeed in them. Such places have a mystique that the media play up, not against. In February 2013, IBM's newly appointed CEO flew into Nairobi to celebrate the newest IBM research center, which is located in Kenya. That month CNN filled the airwaves with images of Kenyan militants made up in whiteface practicing how to machete their opponents to death in the upcoming elections. IBM's research center continues to operate and innovate. The electoral violence never materialized. And even in the most remote places in Africa, you really don't see a lot of people wearing whiteface.

To get past that mystique, I find credibility in firsthand insight. What does the commercial rise of a continent look like to the people driving that rise? What leads to success in a frontier market like Africa, according to the business leaders succeeding there? That is what *Success in Africa* is about.

Africa is big in many ways. It's big geographically, as indicated by the eye-opening map in figure 1–1, created from geospatial data by the digital media legend Kai Krause. Africa is also big in economic activity, from mining to mobile phones; big in resources, especially entrepreneurs and young people; and big in opportunity for both African and global companies. It is also big in challenges, about which I hope this book is candid and sober.

Above all, Africa is big in ambition. If you're interested in frontier markets, growth, and the power of individuals to shape their destiny,

Figure 1–1: The true size of Africa

Source: Kai Krause, provided to Wikimedia Commons, October 11, 2010

you will find value in understanding that ambition and where it leads. And make no mistake: it is Africa's ambition, and no one else's, that leads Africa. Africa is not a place that success is landing on; it is a place creating success for itself and others.

In Africa, there are one hundred fifty $1 billion companies, and more than five hundred with annual sales of $100 million.[2] One rarely hears about them or from their leaders. In the pages that follow, you'll get to know some of those companies, their leaders, and

3

their stories. If you are in global business, investment, or policy, knowing these stories will help inform your work.

Understanding success in Africa has utility, but hopefully offers something more: inspiration. If you believe in the power of people to create their own story, rather than living with the story told about them, you will enjoy *Success in Africa*.

About the Author: West to East to Africa

I navigated to Africa by way of two prior frontier markets: North America and Asia. I was raised in the borough of the Bronx, New York, where the mysteries of the Bo-Sun Chinese restaurant on Johnson Avenue caught my eye as a three-year-old. It was an interest that grew more serious as my horizons and those of Asia opened up. I studied Chinese at Yale and, at age twenty, began working in Asia. As I worked with companies and governments in Taiwan, China, South Korea, Indonesia, Thailand, and elsewhere in the region, I learned what the complete transformation of an economy can look like. It's no accident that there's a small army of Asia alumni active in Africa today. They include not only me, but the head of the *Wall Street Journal* in Africa, the head of GE in Africa, Unilever in Africa, and Cummins in Africa, not to mention the many Asian executives directing Asian companies operating in Africa.

I was far from the earliest to bring my experience to Africa, landing on its shores about ten years ago. To be precise, I landed just off of Africa's shores, on the island of Bioko, part of Equatorial Guinea (EG). At that time, there were only three reasons to be in EG. You were born there, you were launching a coup there, or you were there because of the oil. I was there because of the oil. While working in Asia, I had helped two global oil and gas companies manage their social and economic interactions in remote regions. A U.S.-based company had recently found a natural gas reservoir in EG that was

4

Figure 1–2: Lagos market
Source: Zouzou Wizman, provided to Wikimedia Commons, May 1, 2005.

so large it would transform both the country and the company. A team I led was retained to help the company understand how its massive construction projects could help foster a prosperous, diversified, and stable Equatorial Guinea, still very much a work in progress. I've since undertaken similar projects across Africa, as well as more straightforward strategy assignments. Most of these have been in the company of talented colleagues at Dalberg Global Development Advisors.*

Equatorial Guinea, itself quite sleepy at the time, didn't awaken me to the opportunities prevalent throughout Africa. But my second assignment did, and for keeps. It was in Lagos, Nigeria, one of the largest cities in the world. When you land in Lagos, they don't say

---

*While many of the insights in *Success in Africa* are from work with Dalberg, and other firms, all opinions expressed are strictly my own.

"Welcome to Lagos." They say, "This is Lagos." It's a tough town, and I loved it instantly.

Figure 1-2 is a picture of one of the main markets in Lagos. It says a lot about Africa.*

Some readers may see in this photo only chaos. What I see in this photo is different. I see the opportunity in Africa. I also hear it: the deafening hum of entrepreneurialism; hard, hard work; and belief in the future. I hear at least one hundred people talking on cell phones that, according to World Bank statistics, they could not possibly afford. I hear the voices of mostly young people. Africa has a larger portion of its population entering the workforce than any other region of the world.

The picture is not all bright. I do see what's missing: reliable electricity, roads, health care, education. Their absence causes a lot of human suffering today. However, each of those needs is driving innovation and investment. According to McKinsey and Company, those demands are on a trajectory to create $820 billion in new growth in infrastructure, agriculture, and consumer spending over the twelve years ending in 2020.[3]

The Continent We Can't See

Africa is experiencing a boom that extends from metals to mobile payments. Many assume that the growth is overwhelmingly in natural resources like oil, gas, and mining. Natural resources are a big part of the story. However, as figure 1–3 shows, three-fourths of the story is elsewhere.

---

*Here I'm borrowing the technique of Miles Morland, a private investor in Africa who sits on the board of one of its largest companies. Miles writes an occasionally brutal and always savvy newsletter, and uses a photo of Ghana street life in a similar way.

Sector share of change in real GDP, 2002–07
Percent, 100% = $235 billion[1]

Compound annual
growth rate, %

Sector	Share	Growth rate
Resources	24	7.1
Wholesale and retail	13	6.8
Agriculture	12	5.5
Transport, telecommunications	10	7.8
Manufacturing	9	4.6
Financial intermediation	6	8.0
Public administration	6	3.9
Construction	5	7.5
Real estate, business services	5	5.9
Tourism	2	8.7
Utilities	2	7.3
Other services[2]	6	6.9

1 In 2005 dollars. The total is the sum of 15 countries for which data were available, and that together account for 80 percent of Africa's GDP: Algeria, Angola, Cameroon, Egypt, Ethiopia, Kenya, Libya, Morocco, Nigeria, Senegal, South Africa, Sudan, Tanzania, Tunisia, Zimbabwe.
2 Education, Health, Social Services, Household Services.

Figure 1–3: Africa's growth has been widespread across sectors

Source: *Lions On the Move*, McKinsey Global Institute, June 2010. By permission.

Data like these frame each chapter of *Success in Africa*. But data do not dominate. Story and character do.

Success in Africa focuses on the business leaders building the continent and the insights their careers provide. I've seen quantitative evidence of Africa's growth fail to penetrate the consciousness of many, including business executives deploying global capital. Not long ago, I led a team interviewing thirty top U.S. investors, financial intermediaries, and trade experts about Africa. We asked them how many African companies they thought had $100 million in annual revenue (you will recall the actual figure is more than five hundred). The typical response was between thirty and forty.

That experience resonates with Robert Rubin, former U.S. treasury secretary and previously cochairman of Goldman Sachs. Bob has been interested in Africa since he travelled there as head of the treasury in 1998 and saw growth opportunities that have taken others the better part of the next fifteen years to recognize. He says that today, most still don't. "I can go a year around here," he said, waving a hand to the thousand-odd investment banks and private equity firms visible from his current corner office in midtown New York, "and no one will bring up Africa unless I do."

I had imagined this a uniquely American phenomenon, until I discussed it in the Mayfair section of London with Phuthuma Nhleko. Phuthuma built a telecommunication company in Africa with over $14 billion turnover and in excess of $30 billion market capitalization. He sits on the boards of two of the world's largest companies, BP and Anglo American, both based in London. Phuthuma describes an experience a lot like Bob's and mine:

> If you watch the BBC or CNN or Fox, every day what you see about Africa is disease, problems, poverty, etc. The African middle class and its huge progress and upward mobility is virtually non-existent. This is a crazy omission and misrepresentation to the business and investing community. If you were to take a hundred American or European twenty-five-year-old fund managers and say, "Africa," their response will be "we're not going to bother about that now or this is not a priority. We'll look at other 'emerging markets' like Russia and China. Africa is just a big black box we don't really understand."
>
> On the other hand, if you were to review Nestlé's, Unilever's, or SABMiller's financials and note where their earnings are derived from, a very material portion is earned in Africa. So, you know... one of these perspectives is missing the point.

For those wishing to see the story clearly, it may be helpful to call out some of the lenses that distort our vision of Africa today.

While there are many, three seem to disable us most, and they help explain why a book on the characters and stories of Africa's rise is so useful.

First, there's the preconception of Africa as the embodiment of need. How many of us were compelled to eat our peas because "There are starving children in Africa?" These warnings have a persistent impact on our adult, and even professional, perceptions of Africa. Those perceptions are reinforced by a news media that is quick to report famines but slow to cover successes. By successes I do not mean the occasional ox farmer or microenterprise doing well. They are critical to reducing poverty but of limited interest to a global business audience. I am talking about African businesses that succeed on a large scale, like the companies and individuals who populate this book.

Second, the entertainment sector has built a fortune depicting Africa as a place of happy animals and miserable people. In global entertainment, the only empowered Africans are the Lion King and Idi Amin. Nelson Mandela earned the life due a hero, but only after twenty-seven years in jail. Africans who are not animals, despots, or Nelson Mandela are portrayed as suffering under the heel of poverty, war, and disease. Recall the last two movies you saw with Africans in them. You will see what I mean.

There is a set of readers looking at these first pages who know the Africa story well. I would ask them not to stop reading just yet. Unless you are routinely speaking with African CEOs and global CEOs engaged in Africa, *Success in Africa* should add new insights to your own.

I hope there are also readers of this book who do not have particular interest in Africa, but are interested in what fast-growth, frontier markets look like and how they work. I write on these markets in *Harvard Business Review,* usually drawing on my experiences and those of extraordinary business leaders to deliver insights that are hard to get another way. If you like that, you may like what you read here.

9

I believe in the power of extraordinary people to tell their own story. For that reason, this book reads in part like oral history. While my views are present, I have also sought to get out of the way and let many business leaders succeeding in Africa speak for themselves.

So, for example, if you squint at figure 1–3, you will see that agriculture accounts for 12 percent of Africa's increase in GDP and has a compound annual growth rate of 5.5 percent. No doubt many readers may have already forgotten that sentence. A better way to tell that story—the way I would want to hear it—is the way it's told by one of Africa's agribusiness leaders, Vimal Shah. Here's Vimal on his core business of palm, sunflower, and related oils:

Africa's per capita consumption is about five kilos of edible oils and fats per year, per person. The World Health Organization says that fifteen kilos is what a human body requires. Europeans eat about forty-two kilos, Americans forty-eight kilos. From five kilos, can we go down? No. We can only go up.

How can we go up? African demand is currently met from Indonesia, Malaysia, and the United States. Going forward, do those countries have enough land to feed Africa's next billion people in the next forty years? I just came back from Indonesia, Malaysia, and Singapore. They have no more land. They have cultivated it all. If that is the case, the question is whether that production is going to happen here. And I say it is going to happen here in Africa because we have no choice. It is not because it is sexy to do it, but it is just that we've got no choice—we've got to do it.

As described in chapter 4, Vimal is doing it. His company and others are bringing commercial-scale production to Africa that is redefining how the world will feed itself.

Who's in *Success in Africa*?

One of the myths *Success in Africa* may put to rest is that Africa is populated only with small or medium enterprises (SMEs).* SMEs are an important part of economic growth in Africa, as elsewhere, but focus on these as the only success stories in Africa can leave global business unclear as to whom and how they would engage.

For that reason, *Success in Africa* focuses on African leaders of very large companies—companies like MTN and SABMiller,† both among the more than forty African companies identified as globally competitive by the Boston Consulting Group.[4] You will meet the leaders who grew these companies and hear their perspectives on Africa and on doing business in a fast-growth, frontier market.

Including only the largest African companies would fail to capture all that is happening in Africa and what the global investor or business leader should know. In Africa, as elsewhere, much of the innovation and future growth rest in immature industries with smaller companies. In particular, the advances in African ICT and private equity are exciting, and so this book includes businesses in both sectors, based more on their products, accomplishments, and the insights of their founders than on their size.

You will also find stories of non-African business leaders who have succeeded in Africa. Ultimately, Africa's future rests with African businesses. However, the stories and insights of men like Tullow Oil's Aidan Heavey or the global perspective of leaders like Coca Cola's Neville Isdell and GE's Jeff Immelt also have great value for

---

*There are many definitions of small and medium enterprises. Most are based on the number of employees, and most of those definitions put that number at fewer than 255.

†SABMiller is listed in London and Johannesburg. Its history, culture, and leadership are strongly African, and I concur with BCG's description of it as African.

readers who want to understand the journey from the "developed" to the "developing" world.

As indicated by the subtitle, this is a book about business leaders. This focus on the individual reflects a belief that leadership plays a critical role in the development of companies, countries, continents, and history. These leaders provide a sense of Africa one could not get from anyone else. They are also, to a person, compelling and enjoyable to read about.

The men and women whose perspectives are included here are or have been active CEOs. None is a passive investor and all have built enterprises based on more than inherited wealth. That does not mean every business leader in this book began with nothing (though many did). In Africa, as elsewhere, if you have wealth, position, or education, your chances of success are higher.

Some of the CEOs you will meet are from well-off families, others from families just well enough off to send their boys to good high schools. Some were born with few resources beyond a strong-willed mom. What they have in common is that all pushed far beyond the platform given them. Consider Vimal Shah's comment on success:

I think in Africa success can mean a lot of things. Success means that you have overcome many obstacles. If you have a billion invested in Africa, was it an easy thing or was it a difficult thing to do? Was it innovative? I think the leaders of even small companies would be counted as very successful if they actually had all the odds stacked against them, and they had the "leading edge," where it was difficult to get in there, but they still did it.

All of the participating business leaders have created or grown highly productive, competitive enterprises. I was well advised on this point by author and Oxford economist Paul Collier. Paul offered thoughts early about this book, in particular on the persistent skepticism of foreign investors and global firms towards African businesses. I asked him why he thinks it persists. "They think it's all rent seeking," he said, using the economic term for making a profit without making a product, producing wealth, or otherwise contributing to society. "Show them companies in Africa producing real goods for real value and doing it at scale." *Success in Africa* does that.

Closely tied to the suspicion of rent seeking is the belief that business leaders in Africa succeed only because they have the right connections, especially in government. Strong government relationships are part of success in Africa. That's true in the United States and in many other countries as well, where lobbying, political contributions, and trade associations each represent an accepted path businesses use to enhance returns by engaging government. Many of the business leaders in this book, though not all, have robust relationships with governments. It is one skill among many that have enabled them to build great businesses.

While writing *Success in Africa*, I was challenged many times to define commercial success in Africa. Perhaps no challenge was more powerful than the one presented by an African business leader of tomorrow. In October 2012, the Harvard Business School's Africa Business Club was kind enough to spend time with me to talk about the work in progress. These young men and women are supremely capable and globally savvy. Reflecting on who should be counted a success in Africa, one MBA student from Nigeria put forward this poser:

My question is how do you become successful *in* Africa and also *in the interests of* Africa? You can become a successful African monopolist, right? You can get a concession and you're licensed to import diesel in a country where they need twenty million liters of diesel every day and you're not adding any value. You're just capturing value and creating inefficiencies. Is that what you want your legacy to be or do you want to be the kind of entrepreneur that actually creates jobs, that creates an environment for younger people. Are you someone who creates opportunity for them to thrive and can enable them, can impart knowledge to them?

Can one define success in Africa independent of the interests of Africa? I would not.

Africa is not a charity case and African businesses are not philanthropies. As I argue in chapter 4, the path to future business success in Africa is intertwined with meeting the massive needs of the continent. Social value and shareholder value are not in parallel, they are not "shared," they need not be measured on a double or triple bottom line. For the companies in this book, social value is a critical success factor in their business. Full stop.

Not the Last Book on Africa

I'm a strategy consultant, and it's a hazard of my profession to help clients define what they won't do, or what they choose to leave to others. I hope the paragraphs above express what this book is. It's worth sharing a few words on what it is not.

It is not a comprehensive look at Africa. As the title suggests, it is a look at commercial success in Africa. There continue to be war, disease, and poverty in Africa. There is also, joyfully, success in art, music, science, governance, health, and education. Others will document, celebrate, and critique these.

This is not a 360-degree profile of the participating CEOs. I thought it would be until my blessed publisher, Erika Heilman, showed me several books that purported to do that for various parts of the world. Reading them was like watching paint dry. I thanked her and restructured the book to focus on what you have in front of you now: perspectives on Africa, what works there, and why, from the people who know. Each of the leaders in this book merits a profile or biography, warts and all. If I get to write one, I'll feel fortunate. If you write one, please let me know.

Finally, this book is not finished. We're sharing a story that is still unfolding. Africa is a continent at the dawn of its emergence. There is every reason to believe there is more to come. Stay tuned.

CHAPTER 2

At the Dawn

At last we all speak the same language, and operate from the
same assumptions.

Sam Jonah, CEO, AngloGold Ashanti (1986–2004)

Even most growth countries, they're coming to that leveling off
point. Not Africa.

Graham Mackay, CEO, SABMiller (1999–2012)

Few images convey Africa's turnaround as powerfully as two
covers of *The Economist,* separated by eleven years and depicted in
figure 2–1.

In 2000, the editors of the *Economist* saw in Africa a continent in a
spiral of violence and despair. As the *Economist*'s editors described it in
their lead editorial, "Mozambique and Madagascar have been deluged
by floods, famine has started to reappear in Ethiopia, Zimbabwe has
succumbed to government-sponsored thuggery, and poverty and pes-
tilence continue unabated. Most seriously, wars still rage from north
to south and east to west." It was a damning safari of sorrow, one that
ended fatalistically. "Brutality, despotism and corruption exist everywhere," the *Economist* reported, "but African societies, for reasons
buried in their cultures, seem especially susceptible to them."[1]

May 13, 2000

December 3, 2011

Figure 2–1: *The Economist* on Africa, then and now

Source: *The Economist*. By permission.

What a difference a decade makes.

"From the day I started my job," said John Micklethwait, the *Economist* editor in chief since 2006, "I've heard from people about that hopeless continent cover." He reflected on the legacy of that cover, and the genesis of the starkly different 2011 "Africa Rising" cover article:

> People have gone to great pains to point out to me that if you invested in a basket of African stocks on the day we declared Africa a "hopeless continent" you would be doing quite well today. In 2011, our reporters were writing about the growth of several African countries, and it prompted us to consider whether there was something bigger here to write about. Whenever you run a cover on a big issue, there's a small group that will say, "Well, we've known that for years." There's a much larger group who will see it as new, but then recognize that the trend is all around them. I think that's the case here.

John and his team acknowledged the *Economist*'s dire predictions at the start of the decade. In a striking parallel, their lead editorial in 2011 took a similar tour, and found a continent transformed:

> From Ghana in the west to Mozambique in the south, Africa's economies are consistently growing faster than those of almost any other region of the world. At least a dozen have expanded by more than 6 percent a year for six or more years. Ethiopia will grow by 7.5 percent this year, without a drop of oil to export. Once a byword for famine, it is now the world's tenth-largest producer of livestock... Severe income disparities persist through much of the continent; but a genuine middle class is emerging.[2]

Numerous data pointed to a continent that had spent the last decade and more going in the right direction, including reduced inflation,

Country	2001–10		Country	2011–15
Angola	**11.1**		China	9.5
China	10.5		India	8.2
Myanmar	10.3		**Ethiopia**	**8.1**
Nigeria	**8.9**		**Mozambique**	**7.7**
Ethiopia	**8.4**		**Tanzania**	**7.2**
Kazakhstan	8.2		Vietnam	7.2
Chad	**7.9**		**Congo (DRC)**	**7**
Mozambique	**7.9**		**Ghana**	**7**
Cambodia	7.7		**Zambia**	**6.9**
Rwanda	**7.6**		**Nigeria**	**6.8**

Figure 2–2: Top 10 countries in GDP growth over the past decade and the next five years

Source: Ernst & Young, *Building Bridges: Ernst & Young's 2012 Attractiveness Survey–Africa,* 201. By permission.

budget deficits, and foreign debt. Labor productivity and gross domestic product rose, and continental growth rates projected into the foreseeable future of at least 5 percent on a base of about $2 billion (slightly smaller than Brazil, slightly larger than India or Russia).* Of the ten countries that grew fastest in the decade from 2001 to 2010, six were African. Looking ahead to 2015, that number rises to seven.

External factors like the demand in Asia for raw materials are

---

*Africa is a continent; Brazil, Russia, and India are countries. The comparison is primarily to give the reader a sense of scale. However, as discussed in the following chapter, thinking of Africa holistically has merit.

widely reported and important as driving Africa's growth. Some of these are discussed in chapter 7. However, they do not explain growth in countries that are resource-poor or trading little. CEOs succeeding in Africa provide insight on more internal drivers of growth, decades in the making. Even business leaders in export-driven businesses like oil and mining perceive Africa's growth to date as driven by three forces largely internal to Africa:

- A revolution in governance
- An evolution in education
- A transformation in communications

A Revolution in Governance

The end of the Cold War had a favorable impact that one doesn't hear clearly enough sitting in Western capitals. Cold War politics was like oil or bad aid: an external force the governments of Africa could serve while delivering little for their citizens at home. That's how Sam Jonah remembers it. Sam is the former CEO of AngloGold Ashanti, the first African company to be listed on the New York Stock Exchange. Today he serves on the boards of several public companies and is described by *Forbes* as one of the twenty most influential business figures in Africa.[3] Sam grew up in a Ghanaian mining town and began work below ground, a laborer in the mines he would eventually command. Sam does not mince words about the Cold War and the kind of leader it produced: "Look at Angola. Look at the Congo. Mobutu* was a son of a bitch, but the Americans could feel confident

---

*From 1965–1997, the president of the Congo (which he renamed Zaire). His given name was Joseph Desire' Mobutu, which he also changed while in office to *Mobutu Sese Seko Nkuku Ngbendu Wa Za Banga* ("The all-powerful warrior who, because of his endurance and inflexible will to win, goes from conquest to conquest, leaving fire in his wake").

that he was their son of a bitch, so he stayed in power. That was going on, on both sides, all over the continent."

With the collapse of the Soviet Union the power of socialism as a political force eroded worldwide. Throughout Africa, states adopted some version of market economics (though this ranges widely). As Sam put it, "At last we all began to speak the same language, and operate from the same assumptions."

Phuthuma Nhleko likewise pointed to the Cold War's end as a defining moment in Africa. In particular, he describes the decline and dismembering of the Soviet Union as having created room that ultimately proved helpful to Africa's growth, in parallel to the rise of China and the consequential growth of Chinese demand:

There is no question in my mind that the first and main trigger leading to the turnaround and recent positive developments in Africa was the end of the Cold War. Once the Berlin Wall fell, there wasn't a counterparty to bankroll governments that may have had a very strong socialist agenda. African governments realized they had only one port of call in a singular polar world, which was the U.S. and the West. The very strong left-leaning governments on the continent found themselves in an invidious position where the West could stipulate reform conditions for any aid and financial support. Out of pride, the unpalatable conditions thankfully forced African governments to pursue a path of self-reliance and more financial independence.

Vimal Shah is slightly younger than either Phuthuma or Sam. He built his company in the wake of the change they lived. He sees the path set when the "liberators" retired as inexorable. He discussed it over tea, looking out his office window toward Uganda, where he is creating a seventy-five-thousand-acre palm oil plantation:

Every country in Africa today is reforming, going up the ladder of growth. Those ladders are all looking towards capitalism. I don't see ladders looking towards communism anymore. There are no differences in ideologies now. We all talk the same language, and our officials and business leaders are now educated in many of the same universities.

Bharat Thakrar also sees a steady march away from violence and militancy across Africa, driven by its youth culture. Bharat is the CEO of Scangroup, the largest communications firm in Africa, a partner of global communications leaders such as WPP, Ogilvy, Hill & Knowlton, and Millward Brown. Bharat's historical narrative is informed by the time he spends in focus groups with young African consumers. He sees their aspirations as the ultimate weapon to defeat Mobutu-like leaders in Africa:

My perspective on Africa is that civilization has to go through some pretty tough turning points. If you look at the U.S. you had a civil war and then you had two world wars, and then recently had your huge terrorist attack. If you look at China and India they had socialist or communist revolutions. Russia the same thing. Europe? Two world wars. Human society has to go through those huge turning points and I think in Africa's case it's post-colonialism. Every country on the continent has been through a trauma, including military dictators and civil war.

So, what does it mean that "Africa is rising" today? I think the correct meaning is the literal one, that we have now awakened. We've been through the shit and can look at ourselves optimistically. If you talk to young consumers today in any country on the continent—Nigeria, Mozambique, Angola—there is a sense of pride, a commitment to leave behind all this nonsense of

political and militant dictatorship. That's why you have democratization and that is why the military separatist movements
today have no room to survive. If you ask a young African about
Al Shabaab or the Boko Haram,* "Do you think these guys have
got any legs?" they will tell you to forget it, it's not going to happen. Younger people are fed up with it.

Bharat's optimism is shared widely among CEOs. Not all the data support it, and the picture is a nuanced one. Instability and violence persist.
The Global Peace Index (GPI), produced by the Institute for Economics
and Peace, ranked the Democratic Republic of the Congo, Sudan, and
Somalia among its five least peaceful countries.[4] As this book was being
drafted, Mali and the Central African Republic both experienced coups.

Having said that, Africa as a whole has experienced an increase in
stability and a substantial decline in the number of major armed con-
flicts.[5] As indicated in figure 2–3, conflict has dropped in waves. West
Africa's stabilization began in the early 1990s. In North Africa, that
trend began around 2000, though there was a recent spike with the
Arab Spring. East Africa has experienced steady stabilization since
2000. Southern Africa began the transition in the early 1980s and it
accelerated in the early 2000s.[6]

While these nuances are significant, they should not obscure the
fundamental insight that conflict is going down. It's trend of which
it is easy to lose sight in the wake of news. A leading Silicon Valley
investor interested in Africa's emerging technology sector recently
sent me a graphic he found in a British newspaper showing all the
secessionist movements in Africa and what the map would look like if
they all succeeded. The paper did its readers a terrible disservice with
that graphic, as it would if it sounded alarms about the secessionist

---

*Al Shabaab and Boko Haram are militant movements based in Somalia and
Nigeria respectively.

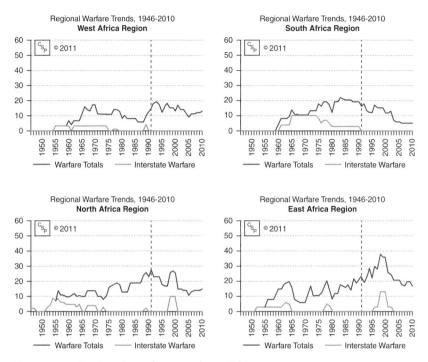

Figure 2–3: Regional warfare trends in Africa

Source: The Center for Systemic Peace, *Global Conflict Trends*. October 2012. By permission.

movements in Texas, California, and New York City, all of which have threatened to leave the United States. While some coups succeed, they are few, and getting fewer, as figure 2–4 demonstrates.

With a reduction in coups has come government that is perceived by many business leaders to be more responsive and more democratic. That perception requires some nuance, and not everyone would agree. Many see freedom in Africa moving too slowly, and even backward in countries like Nigeria, Ethiopia, and Rwanda, which have experienced consolidation of power in the hands of long-ruling parties and presidents. Progress toward responsive government in Africa has been uneven. However, the direction over time is clear, and its impact on business is clearer still.

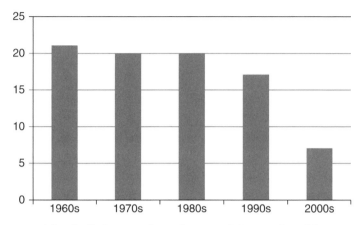

Figure 2–4: The declining number of successful coups in Africa

Source: Data from *The Economist, Africa's year of elections: The democracy bug is fitfully catching.* Jul 22, 2010.

Today, all countries in Africa, with the exception of Eritrea, hold elections. Elections are where the story of freedom and responsive government starts, not where it ends. The Polity IV Project measures political regime traits to assess the extent of a government's democratic nature.* The score represents a spectrum of governing authority from fully institutionalized autocracies (low scores) through mixed authority regimes to fully institutionalized democracies (high scores). Figure 2–5 shows the trend across Africa since 1990.

Freedom is not just measured by sound elections, but a liberal environment before and after elections. The non-governmental organization Freedom House assesses that environment using a broad set of indicators including political rights and civil liberties. Freedom House standards are high, classifying countries such as Turkey and

---

*The score is built using key qualities of executive recruitment, constraints on executive authority, and political competition as well as changes in the institutionalized qualities of governing authority. The "Polity Score" captures this regime authority spectrum on a 21-point scale ranging from –10 (hereditary monarchy) to +10 (consolidated democracy).

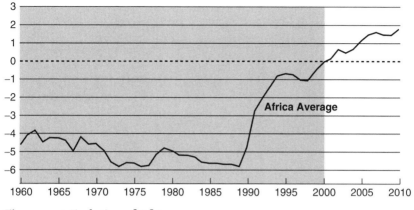

Figure 2–5: Evolution of African governance

Source: Data from Polity IV, as reported in Ernst & Young, *2012 Attractiveness Survey – Africa*. By permission.

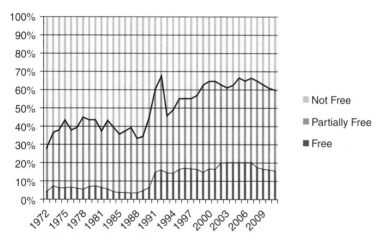

Figure 2–6: Ratings of 54 African countries by Freedom House

Source: Freedom House: *Freedom in the World,* 2012. By permission.

Colombia as "partially free." Figure 2–6 shows Africa's performance on the Freedom House index over time.

It should be noted that the past several years are not as heartening as the longer-term trend. The same Freedom House measure that shows longer-term progress indicates that the number of sub-Saharan full "electoral democracies" fell from twenty-four in 2005 to nineteen in 2012.[7] The Ibrahim Index, a benchmark governance measure specifically for Africa, indicates a 5 percent decline in African political participation since 2007.

Acknowledging that democracy is far from being fully evolved in Africa, Phuthuma Nhleko has seen the impact of the existing level of democratization on business. Before joining the BP and Anglo American corporate boards, Phuthuma earned his credibility by building MTN, Africa's largest mobile operator, with $14 billion in annual revenue and a market capitalization of over $30 billion from operations in more than twenty-one countries in Africa and the Middle East. Across Africa's markets, he describes more responsive governance and a direct relationship between that responsiveness and success for his business:

From a business perspective, Africa is on a recognizable, discernible evolution from military-style governments, where we experienced frequent coups in some parts of the continent, to some form of democracy no matter how imperfect it may be. Imperfect democracies come with a much higher degree of transparency and accountability than any military junta or dictatorship. That accountability helps to usher in and underpin the entire market economy. We experienced this during MTN's entrance into Nigeria amongst a number of other countries.

Nigeria is a useful example because it has all the elements of what I'm trying to convey. Before privatization of the telecoms sector in Nigeria, the country had six hundred thousand fixed lines for a population of over 120 million people. You often had to wait several months for your new line to be connected. You had to spend thousands of dollars to get on the waiting list. The elections in Nigeria, even if imperfect, resulted in a civilian government and the commencement of a privatization process. Fast-forward to today, what was once six hundred thousand lines is now over 70 million lines. To say that the Nigerian telecom sector has undergone evolution is an understatement.

The reduction in coups and the transition (albeit uneven) to democracy contribute to broader business confidence in Africa. Polling of business leaders by the global professional services firm PricewaterhouseCoopers shows CEOs in African markets more confident about growth than their global counterparts.[8]

On a more granular level, the African business community's confidence in governance is seen in the way companies approach longterm planning. In Kenya, for example, every election used to mean a complete rearrangement of the economy. Each new officeholder doled out portions of the economy to his patronage network. Regular reshuffling of the economic deck scrambled business confidence. You could see it in the cyclical shrinkage of the want ads before each election.

Patronage is not gone from Kenya, but its impact is much diminished. Today, the country's economic development is guided by Vision 2030, a strategy with broad support from business, government,

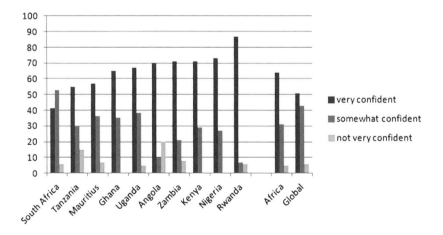

Figure 2–7: Confidence in Africa's growth potential

Source: PricewaterhouseCoopers, *The Africa Business Agenda*, July 2011. By permission.

and civil society, articulated in specific projects and actions that are not expected to change with each election. The effect is palpable for men like James Mworia, CEO of Centum Investments, the largest quoted investment company in East Africa listed on the Nairobi Stock Exchange. Compact and athletic, Mworia moves about his Nairobi office with energy, as if he might burst forth from his tailored shirt. He is specific and sharp. "I'll give you a practical example of the effect 2030 has," he said, pulling out documents from both Vision 2030 and the specifications for Two Rivers, a planned mixed-use commercial development being developed by Centum. "Vision 2030 calls for certain key infrastructure projects. The projects they said they would build, they have built. When we wanted to build Two Rivers, we looked at the map of the new infrastructure. Because the plan is now credible, we were able to raise financing. Earlier today, I was having a discussion with one of the hotel operators we want to attract. I was able to show him a presentation from the permanent secretary* in the Ministry of Roads, on the new road network in Nairobi. First of all, that document exists—people know what the plan is. Then, you can see this is what has happened already, this is what is in progress, this is what is planned for. It enables me to have that conversation in confidence."

That kind of confidence in government is a revolution. The $150 million committed to date to Two Rivers exemplifies what such confidence can create.

An Evolution in Education

In the wake of liberation, Africa had a paucity of formal education on every level. At independence, no colony had more than 60 percent of the elementary school–age population in school, and most had less

---

*In a parliamentary system, the top technocrat in the ministry; permanent secretaries (PSs) often span the term of several ministers.

than 30 percent; the percentages were even lower for high school and tertiary education. On the day of liberation in the Congo, a country of fifteen million,[9] there were exactly fifty university graduates.[10]

Today, many Africans in both public and private leadership positions have studied abroad. That history can be seen in a few of the business leaders who participated in this book. In chronological order, Sam Jonah went to the Camborne School to study mining, Phuthuma Nhleko to Ohio State to study civil engineering, Funke Opeke to Columbia to study engineering, and Dalberg's James I. Mwangi* went to Harvard to study economics.

At the generational level, Phuthuma observed that increased levels of education changed not only the quality of African leadership, but its very sense of purpose and identity:

You must remember that Africa was, in a number of respects, stuck in the vestiges of a colonial time warp until the early 1990s. The dominant leadership in Africa post-independence was quite understandably revolutionary and radical in its thinking in what was then a less complex bi-polar world. The newly independent African countries sent young people overseas, some of them to the best colleges in the world. After the early '90s, Africa began to reap the full benefits of this act as the returnees entered into government and started businesses. Some of them went to the likes of Stanford and Harvard and other prestigious universities in Western and Eastern Europe. Invariably, the more educated younger generation of African

---

* Fortunately for this world, there are at least two James Mwangis, both mentioned in *Success in Africa*. One is the CEO of Equity Bank, the other the general managing partner of Dalberg. They get each other's e-mails routinely from senders including me. For clarity, and in deference to his seniority, I will refer to the Equity Bank CEO as James Mwangi, the Dalberg GMP as James I. Mwangi.

leaders hold a different worldview from the prior generation. So when a multinational corporation enters Africa and says, "Listen, we can do this and that for you," the African governments they're engaging are exceedingly more sophisticated with a more educated management class than thirty years ago. The governments will retort that "actually, this is what we want and this is how you should provide it."

Today the executive branch in many African countries is being staffed by thirty- and forty-year-olds who have been out in the world. As an example, Mozambique has a significantly more educated and sophisticated civil service corps than at liberation, with people who are committed to changing Mozambique's prospects for the better. They operate with a much stronger sense of how they see themselves in the world. They feel that global companies must come and talk to Africans on our terms. It's not us being totally grateful for them coming in, and saying, "I'm going to do this and that for you or for the benefit of your Head of State. Be eternally grateful for that." That attitude of being eternally grateful for the multinationals' mere interest in the country is a mind-set that is no longer prevalent and is only evident in limited circumstances.

James I. Mwangi has a similar perspective. He sees the opportunity to study abroad as not only having expanded his horizons but as a small part of a more fundamental generational shift in Africa:

When I went to the U.S. consulate to say I wanted to apply to universities in the U.S. they gave me some brochures for perfectly good state schools. When I told them I wanted to apply to Harvard and the like, they said they were unaware of anyone getting into those schools from Kenya. Now, I don't expect an official sitting in Nairobi to know every admission into U.S.

schools. It was, though, consistent with a mind-set many Africans have even of themselves, of limited possibility and sort of knowing your place. The truth is that Kenyans have been going to Ivy League schools for decades and we are now there and returning in meaningful numbers. It's part of a much larger story of Africans recognizing larger ambitions, because there are proof points of what is possible. It changes the expectations of ourselves and our governments.

Africa has also been educating its population better at home. Africa is investing in education, with 20 percent of government spending going to education, almost twice the OECD's 11 percent. This investment is beginning to pay dividends, with primary school enrollment increased from 62 percent in 1999 to 76 percent in 2008.[11] Secondary school enrollment went from 25 percent to 35 percent over the same period.[12] Completion rates for primary education in Africa are rising faster than anywhere else in the world.[13]

One proud product of African schools is entrepreneur and philanthropist Tony Elumelu. Tony built United Bank of Africa into a nineteen-country powerhouse. He is now chairman of Heirs Holdings, a proprietary investment company, and of Transcorp, a publicly traded conglomerate that this year entered into a memorandum of understanding with GE to revamp Nigeria's largest power plant. Tony relied on African schools for his own education, and draws his team largely from today's graduates, as he explains:

The standard in university in Nigeria was very high. The expectations were high. You had people who were going out in the world from those schools and excelling at the IMF, in literature, and in business, like me. We used to laugh a little bit, actually, at people who went to the U.S., because they were taking the easy way out. Today most of the people I work with are locally

trained and meeting or exceeding expectations. There are challenges in the schools, of course, but we are working on them,
with training and cultural change.

Neville Isdell, who moved to Zambia with his family at the age
of ten, went on to become the CEO of Coca-Cola. He can trace the
change in education of the professional class from his youth to today.
"The colonial era had left behind very few well-educated people.
There had been a deficit of education," Neville recalls. "That's three
generations ago. Today, it is totally different. I recently addressed
a group of 150 young professionals, all under forty-five, in Dar es
Salaam. I recall thinking 'this is a great, substantive dialogue.' If I'd
closed my eyes, I could have been anywhere in the world. It would not
have been better than there in Dar."

The expanding set of educated Africans does not go unnoticed by
those negotiating with them. Aidan Heavey is the CEO of Tullow Oil,
a company focused on Africa with a string of exploration finds that is
the envy of the sector worldwide. Aidan's are among the highest-stake
negotiations on the continent. "I've noticed in the last thirty years a
huge difference in the education system in Africa and the people that
you're dealing with, an enormous difference," Aidan reflects, "Today
you'll be sitting across the table from somebody and learn the man's
been to Oxford, Cambridge, and Harvard and speaks six languages. I
barely speak English."

Transformation in Communications

The adoption of the mobile phone is the most important technological event in Africa's modern history. In terms of growth and income
levels, it is comparable only to the Green Revolution's impact on India
in the 1960s. The pace of adoption has been astonishing, as shown
in figure 2–8. Africa has picked up mobile telephone use almost

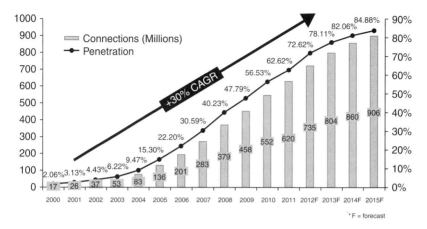

Figure 2–8: Total African mobile connections and penetration rate (million, % penetration)

Source: GSMA Wireless Intelligence, African Mobile Observatory, 2011. By permission.

entirely since 2000. In just seven years, 266 million connections were added. Today, that number has more than tripled

While its effects are on businesses small and great, the mobile revolution is especially pronounced on the productivity and earning potential of individuals and small businesses. Vimal Shah reflects on two everyday occurrences that demonstrate this transformation:

I see the effect every day on my driver. To bring money home to his family and come back, he used to spend a fortune. Going and coming back meant three or four days not working. Today, he does it with one text message. He does not miss work, and he saves all the unnecessary travel expenses. Then consider the vegetable-vendor system here. The vegetables are sold by women who hawk their wares house to house. They would go to the wholesale market, collect a whole bunch of vegetables, and go house to house shouting, "Anybody want to buy vegetables?" Today they have mobile phones. Their customers know their phones. So the lady of the house will ring and say, "I want one kilo of tomatoes. I want this, this, and this." The vegetable woman will purchase just those goods from the market, deliver straight to the home, and get paid through the mobile phone. Imagine the amount of wastage there must have been going around house to house. Now it's gone. It's not required anymore.

Those two stories, multiplied by the 800 million cell phones in Africa today, give you a concrete picture of how the entire continent is recreated by this one technology.[14]

Connectivity has transformed not only small businesses but large ones as well, like Vimal's own. Bidco was well established before he ever held a cell phone. It imported edible oils into Kenyan ports, processed them, and sold oil-based products in the country. That was the extent of Bidco's operation. Vimal's ambition was far more vast. Today his company operates throughout East Africa, serving a market of 140 million consumers. Vimal is unambiguous about what allows him to compete beyond his own borders: cheap and abundant phone service:

What it is doing is changing our speed of business. I am able to speak anytime to my managers in Uganda, Tanzania, anywhere. And when I travel, it is no problem for them to connect with me. A mobile phone call from here to the U.S. costs the same as what it costs for me to call the next-door office.* To call China it is the same, and to India, even less. Before, we had two hundred thousand landlines in Kenya and as a nation we were unsuccessful, totally. Now we have eighteen million mobile phones, in a population of forty million. It removes the lack of communication that was holding us back.

---

*At the time of this writing, a mobile phone call from Nairobi to New York costs $0.03 per minute.

Because mobile phones are so ubiquitous, their capabilities are being stretched and reinvented in Africa. The most notable example is mobile payment. Throughout Africa, a credit card (and for the most part, credit itself) is a luxury of the rich. Cash transactions are limiting and potentially dangerous. Mobile banking allows customers to send money to family and merchants via either prepaid credit on their phones or direct transfers between accounts. In 2011, Vimal's driver and vegetable merchant were two of the more than forty million who multiplied their productivity through mobile payments.[15]

It's hard to overstate how deeply mobile phones have penetrated Africa. In 2007, I worked with the Nigerian army's chief of staff as he negotiated early ceasefires with antigovernment militant commanders. The militant camps were deep in the creeks of the Niger Delta, unreachable by the government and far off any grid. Each antigovernment militant commander had a cell phone, and they would call each other (and also call the Army Chief of Staff, who had them on speed dial). In 2010, I worked on a mining project 400 miles inland from an already remote capital. It took a charter plane and three hours of unpaved road to get to the surrounding villages, nestled deep in mountainous territory. Everyone in those villages has access to a cell phone. Whether they are using it to get crop information or just to call their sons in the capital, that phone means their world is not limited to a day's walk.

Mobile phones and connectivity are often described as "leapfrogging" technologies, because they leap over earlier technologies. Working in Africa and other frontier markets, I've found "leapfrog" technology has a meaning that runs deeper. The fact that cell phone technology leaps over the landline technology I used growing up in the Bronx doesn't much matter to an African, or to African growth. What's really meaningful is that it has allowed men and women in Nairobi, the Niger Delta, and that remote mining community to leap over the miles separating them, the boundaries of their previous lives, and the constraints of what they could be. That is the leap that has unleashed a torrent of productivity and opportunity in Africa.

Is It Still Morning?

So much growth has occurred in Africa in the last decade, some might wonder whether the future continues to be as bright. Quantitative data and CEO insight each indicates some confidence.

For businesses looking for growth, the world's heat map is stark. Figure 2–9 shows where growth is expected over the next five years, based on Ernst & Young's compilation of public and proprietary data.

Each of the internal drivers of growth in Africa to date is expected to continue. But there is one mega-driver whose impact has not yet been felt, and which business leaders all point to: demographics.

Africa has the youngest population in the world. Four out of ten Africans are below the age of fifteen. The median age is twenty. Today, that means a very high portion of Africa's population is dependent on the adult workforce. Tomorrow, however, it means that the workforce will be massive, and the ratio of dependents to workers (the dependency ratio) will be the lowest in the world.

That trend is not without challenges, including training that workforce to meet the needs of the twenty-first century. However, most businesses and investors looking at the youth bulge see it as a massive driver of growth and opportunity. Emerging markets investment pioneer and Templeton Vice Chair Mark Mobius writes about Africa in his "Investing in the Cradle of Civilization" blog series. He describes this "great African resource: a huge and youthful population" as a key rationale for investing there.[16]

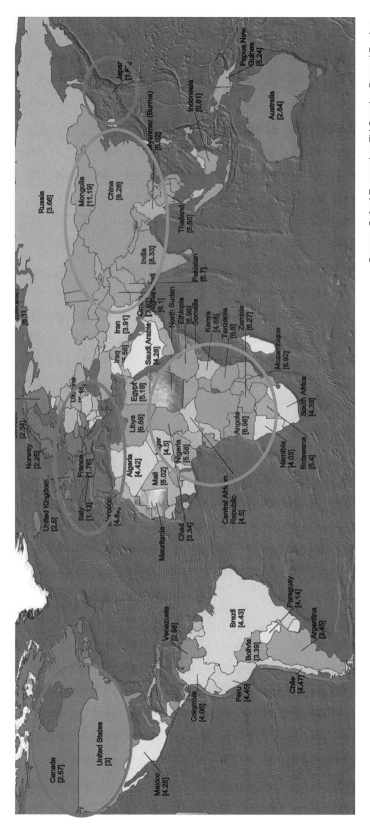

Figure 2–9: Five-year global outlooks for combined annual growth of GDP (November 2012)

Source: Ernst &Young, *Africa CEO Forum Presentation*. November 2012. By permission.

Source: Oxford Economics; EY Growing Beyond Borders

That confidence is shared by other global business leaders familiar with Africa. General Electric has more than $150 billion in revenue with a market capitalization of about $240 billion, making it the sixth-largest company in the Fortune 500. CEO Jeff Immelt sees enough opportunity in Africa to move the needle for his company. In 2011 he established an Africa business unit and installed one of GE's top dozen executives, Jay Ireland, as the first CEO of the unit. Jay has held previous leadership positions in GE Plastics, NBC, and, most recently, was CEO of GE Asset Management, which oversees more than $120 billion in assets. He hardly needed the job of CEO Africa. I asked Jay why he took it.

"I didn't just take the job," he said. "I sought out Jeff and told him I wanted it. We're in the nascent phase with Africa. A lot of what is happening here now is reminiscent of what I saw in China when I worked there in the early 1990s. I remember being struck that the vice premier of China at that time went to Wharton. No one before him had that kind of background. It was guys like that that built the country, and you're just beginning to see that in Africa now."

Jay's perspective is that opportunity is just beginning to open up in Africa for international and domestic firms alike. "The biggest opportunities are yet to come," he says. "The inflection point will be in the confidence of investors and businesspeople, combined with government policies that create a good business environment at the regional level. That combination will produce a tipping point here. It's not here yet. It's coming."

Growth is prone to make a continent thirsty. London-based SABMiller is one of the world's largest brewers, the maker of Miller, Pilsner Urquell, Fosters, and more than 150 other brands yielding $31 billion in global revenue and a market capitalization of about $54 billion. Executive Chairman Graham Mackay explained that "Fifteen years ago we set up an Africa business unit. In those fifteen years, we have had only two in which the Africa unit did not deliver double-digit growth in U.S. profits." Today emerging Africa accounts for 13 percent of SABMiller's earnings.[*,17] Graham only sees that figure growing:

There is a long, long runway ahead. The consumption levels for our products are so low that they've got to rise. You don't find that in most of the world. In fact, there's almost nowhere else in the world where you can say that. Even in Latin America it's not true. Beer consumption in Africa, outside of South Africa, is below ten liters per person per year. The average for Latin America is probably four times that. In the U.S. it is eighty liters. Here in the U.K. it would be eighty-five or ninety. But Africa is at ten. Then you take cultural factors into account, and the rate of growth of the population, and there is much more potential in Africa than there is anywhere else in the world.

"Most everything grows on an S curve," Graham concluded, drawing the curve with his fingertip on the table. "There's slow early adoption, then it really takes off and then when it's bigger it begins to taper. For us, most countries of the world are at the top," he says, running his finger along the flattening line. "Even most growth countries, they're coming to that leveling off point. Not Africa."

Graham's finger moved back down the curve, tapping right where the steepest growth starts. "This is Africa."

---

* Unless otherwise specified, earnings refers to earnings before interest, taxes, depreciation, and amortization, or EBITDA

CHAPTER 3

Becoming Africa

Once Rwanda hit the airwaves, I knew we were in trouble. We were all Rwanda.

Sam Jonah, CEO, AngloGold Ashanti (1986–2004)

Whenever I meet somebody from Africa, they will come to me as an African.

Mo Ibrahim, CEO, Celtel (1998–2005)

Is there "an Africa"?

How you answer defines not just how success in Africa is described but how it is achieved. Businesses falter in Africa because they fail to distinguish its parts, and because they fail to grasp its whole. There are the beginnings of a whole Africa today, and more of a whole Africa tomorrow. Africa is becoming.

Africa Has Parts: See Them

Africa is an exceptionally diverse continent. Much attention is paid to the different governing systems between former French and British colonies, but that is only the first layer of diversity. Across fifty-four states, Africa today has six official languages born of its colonial

43

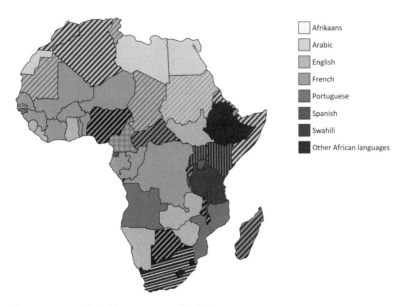

Figure 3–1: Official languages of Africa

Source: NordNordWest, provided to Wikimedia July 14, 2011.

history and the migration of Islam. Preceding these are hundreds of distinct ethnolinguistic and tribal groups, many of which do not correspond to national boundaries. In addition to these tribal differences, Africa is religiously diverse, with both Abrahamic and traditional faiths having significant influence.

If you approach Africa as an undifferentiated whole, you approach it at your peril. Scangroup's Bharat Thakrar grows livid about the mistakes made by international firms with a single marketing approach for all of Africa:

Why do global companies make a mistake when entering Africa that they would never make elsewhere? You've got to be able to communicate to the consumers in a language the consumer understands. When you go to Europe do you look at Europe as

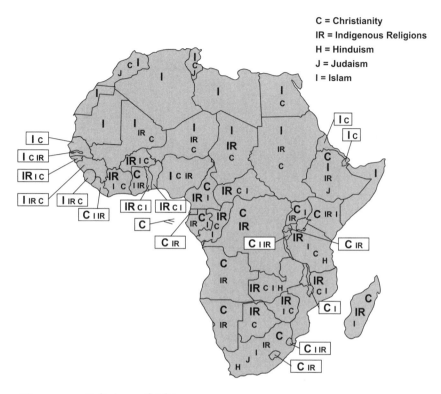

C = Christianity
IR = Indigenous Religions
H = Hinduism
J = Judaism
I = Islam

Figure 3–2: Religions of Africa

Source: Central Intelligence Agency, Washington, D.C.

one market? You know the Italian is very different from the Spanish, the Spanish is very different from the French, so you don't want to create a single communication and blast it out to them.

They do that to Africa thinking all Africans are idiots. Africans are not idiots; they see themselves or they do not see themselves. A Tanzanian will look at an ad and will say, "I don't see myself there. That's a Kenyan, that's a South African there, so that's not for me." The communication does not meet with them, so they do not buy your product.

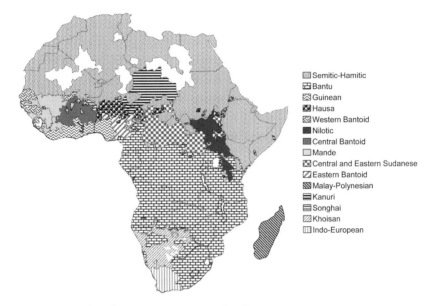

Figure 3–3: Ethnolinguistic groups and tribes
Source: Central Intelligence Agency, Washington, D.C.

Africans are long used to others painting the continent with a single brushstroke. It obscured the nascent success in Africa, in particular when the brush tip was dipped in blood.

Sam Jonah experienced that effect firsthand when raising capital for AngloGold Ashanti. In 1996, Sam had come to New York to pitch the company to U.S. investors. He was CEO of the largest gold mining company in the world, with a low cost structure and favorable price forecasts for its product. Sam had just led the company's listing on the New York Stock Exchange, making it the first African company on the Big Board. The trip was to be a routine follow-up to the listing. It wasn't routine. That week, the Rwandan genocide filled the airwaves with images of African rivers choked with bodies and African faces distorted in rage. The nightly news was a window into a horrifying dystopia emerging in real time.

Sam knew what was happening in Rwanda would reflect on him, and on home. "Most investors then still thought Africa was a country," he recalled, "one country. When we did our road show for the listing, no matter how many times we told the investors our operations were in Ghana, they thought we were in Guyana, or Guinea. And once Rwanda hit the airwaves, I knew we were in trouble. We were all Rwanda."

Sam had spent a lifetime moving his company, and Africa, away from such images. He was born in the town where Ashanti Goldfields (the predecessor to the current AngloGold Ashanti) had its largest mine, and Sam was raised in the mine's shadow. His father was a contractor by trade, and built his business up sufficiently to send his boys to school in Ghana. Against his parents' wishes, Sam went into mining and won the attention of the mine manager, who recommended him for a corporate scholarship to study for a certificate in mining in the U.K. He returned to Ashanti and climbed the organization chart into levels few black Africans had obtained. In 1986, at the age of thirty-six, he became the company's first black CEO, and its youngest. In 1995 he successfully listed the company on the New York Stock Exchange.[1] He then spent the better part of the following year trying to recover from the events in Rwanda—a country where his company had no operations, and where he himself had never been. It was an object lesson in where Africa stood at the time.

The risk of the red brush is still real. In 2012, as this book was being completed, Mali experienced a coup and subsequent insurgency. In the short term, it was reasonable for business confidence to falter...in Mali. However, the falter extended, with little real justification, to all of Africa. An editor at a major global news organization wondered aloud to me whether Africa was "headed back to the bad old days." We still seem just one event away from painting Africa with a single brush.

Seeing the Parts Is Not Enough

For both Africa and the businesses hoping to succeed there, it makes sense to be aware of its parts. It also makes sense to look at the whole.

While first considering *Success in Africa,* I had a casual conversation with a friend, Jeff Walker. Jeff founded and led CCMP, a private equity firm with $12 billion in assets under management. Under Jeff's leadership CCMP had entered Europe at the dawn of its private equity market and had prospered. "I liked it," he said. "You had all these managers who were under-incented, because all they could do was make money for the owners of the companies. Private equity guys like us showed up and said they could be the owners. If that could happen in Africa, that'd be great."

CCMP did not invest in Africa while Jeff was CEO and is not invested in Africa today. I asked Jeff how he would look at investment in Africa. "The first thing you're going to look at as an investor going overseas is market size," he said. "Is there enough scale there to make the transaction worthwhile? Europe became interesting because of European integration. Does that exist in Africa?"

It does. In 2000, Tom Gibian founded private equity firm Emerging Capital Partners (ECP) to help bring the model to Africa. Tom's a committed Quaker who trained at Wharton and cut his teeth at Goldman Sachs. He has a strong sense of personal mission, but it never gets in the way of objective financial analysis. Recalling the premise on which ECP was founded, he commented, "We saw that there was no shortage of human capacity and entrepreneurial opportunity in Africa, but there was a shortage of capital and technology. That was—and is—a promising equation." Tom invested in the likes of Sam Jonah and telecoms pioneer Mo Ibrahim when few others would. ECP is among the earliest private equity firms to enter Africa. Others have come in since, and in 2011, investors closed $3 billion-worth of private equity deals.[2]

The principal challenge Tom saw, and still sees, in Africa is fragmentation. "The biggest problem this continent has is too many countries," Tom said.

Former treasury secretary and Goldman Sachs head Bob Rubin sees the challenge in historical perspective, considering what it took for investors to see opportunity in other frontier markets. "You, know, I saw Mexico change investor perceptions around, mostly with road shows of large companies," he said. "I've seen Spain do it as well. I don't think Africa can replicate that because they have few countries that are large enough for that.* Most businesses looking at where to go next, they derail the small countries for the most part. So to approach the many small countries of Africa on a national basis may not work for most businesses."

It's a challenge seen not only by global investors looking at Africa, but by Africans themselves. There are few business leaders more respected in Africa than Mohamed Ibrahim. A native of Sudan, Mo immigrated to London and launched a highly profitable and stable engineering firm serving European mobile operators. He sold that company to do what no European operator would, though he begged them: start an African cell phone company. Seven years after starting it, Mo sold the cell phone company, Celtel, for 3.4 billion dollars.

I met Mo while working on the Natural Resource Charter, a project to reform natural resources development† in Africa. When I told him I wanted his help writing a book on what success looks like in Africa, he stopped me short. He knew what he wanted to focus on:

You talk about Africa; we have fifty-four countries. That is a problem. European countries can act as a bloc, can force company behavior and be a force on the world stage. That is difficult

---

*When Bob and I discussed cross-border projects like the LAPSSET corridor in East Africa, he saw far greater potential to generate investor interest.

† naturalresourcecharter.org.

for Africa. China, Europe, North America, Brazil: these are the blocs that control power, and they do it because they are blocs. If you are not of that size, nobody cares. Do you know why China is where it is, and Africa is not? Because China is one. If we were one, we too would be there. That's why regional integration is essential for Africa to really have a place at the table.

You can't enter new global markets without looking at nations. National-level market analysis and strategy makes sense but it has limits. It makes sense because you need to understand the governance of the country, the political system, the strengths of contracts and the courts, and of course the legal system as it affects setting up, operating, drawing profits from, and shutting down a business. These are *de rigueur* analyses that are essential in new market entry.

However, if a national lens were the only, or even the primary, lens through which you looked at Africa, you would miss it. Almost none of the successful business leaders interviewed in this book is satisfied to work within the bounds of even the largest national markets of Africa. With the advent of technology and a gradual opening of trade, they do not have to.

Consider Regions

One reasonable way to segment African opportunities is by regional trading bloc. There are five key regional blocs in Africa, which are the active Regional Economic Communities (RECs) of the African Economic Community, an organization to promote mutual economic development among African states: The five are:

- SADC (the Southern African Development Community)
- COMESA (the Common Market for Eastern and Southern Africa)

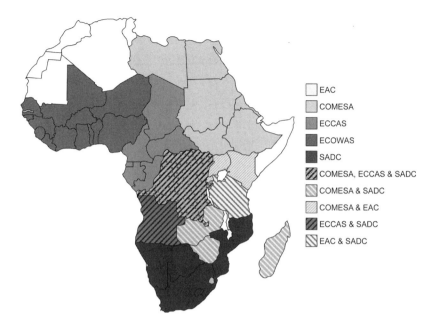

Figure 3–4: Map of trade agreements

Source: Wiz9999, provided to Wikimedia November 5, 2012.

- EAC (the East African Community)
- ECOWAS (the Economic Community of West African States)
- ECCAS (the Economic Community of Central African States)*

Some successful businesses approach African regions serially. Vimal Shah's Bidco is among these. An advocate of owning one's own supply chains, Vimal's eye is squarely focused on where markets are coming together as a whole. "In the East Africa community, we are 140 million people," he said. "By 2050 we will be 250 million. If I can source, produce, and sell in that market, that is a lot of room for

---

* North Africa is included in two RECs that are not currently active, the Community of Sahel-Saharan States (CEN-SAD) and the Arab Maghreb Union (AMU or UMA)

growth." Vimal sees less appeal in some of the other trading blocs in Africa: "You have got ECOWAS in West Africa where free trade is not happening. And North Africa doesn't have a free trade agreement apart from COMESA."

Funke Opeke sees a similar opportunity on the west side of Africa, despite the absence of a functioning free trade regime. Funke is the CEO of Main One Cable Company, a firm that raised and invested $240 million to build a subsea broadband cable to West Africa. When I asked African business school students which CEOs they most admire, Funke was identified repeatedly. When I asked why, they cited her success leading a large project to completion, and her vision to achieve more. The Main One cable first landed in Ghana and Nigeria, two markets that offer extensive growth opportunities on their own. Funke nonetheless expresses her vision in regional terms:

We built the system with a whole-of-West Africa vision. The region has a shared set of development challenges and potential for growth with broadband. We think the rest, especially the southern tip of the continent, is particularly well served now. When we brought the cable to Togo, they had yet to gain access to any cable system directly. Now Togo provides access for us to some of the landlocked countries. It is the same with Benin, where they've had some challenges with the existing broadband and the country is not well connected to the Internet. I'm heading for Senegal on Monday, trying to work with the new government to see if indeed we can complete the line they need to Senegal. We've always wanted to be not just a Nigerian or Ghanaian company and with the kind of infrastructure we have, we're able to leverage it across the region. There's a lot of migration across the region; there's a lot of commonality of culture.

For Centum's James Mworia, the value of focusing on a single region is not so much market size as information asymmetry. Through this focus, he can see and capture opportunities that others can't.

"We are asking the right questions at the regional level first," James says, "where we have the relationships and where the market is naturally coming together. We ask, 'How do we reduce transport cost within this region? How do we share infrastructure such as power?' Kenya is now importing power from Ethiopia. That is where we see our opportunity in the immediate term. Once we have the (East African Community) region, we can then say, 'How do we cooperate with SADDC? If it is not happening at the regional level, it's unlikely to happen at a Pan-African level.'"

That triple lens of proximity, opportunity, and relationship is a powerful advantage of a single-region strategy. It allows a company to take on opportunities in places where others fear to tread, like South Sudan. Recently independent and emerging from a 2005 comprehensive peace agreement (CPA), South Sudan is a locus of active investment from the rest of East Africa. James Mworia is among those investing there. "We took our insurance company into South Sudan in 2005. It was even before the CPA was signed, but we have a good understanding of the market and we've been in the market. We made about $1 million in profit the first year, in insurance of all things."

A tight focus at the regional level also allows James's company to perceive more granular opportunities at the subnational level. He cites the Two Rivers development as an example. "We recently got the results of a market survey that was looking at the purchasing power of the primary retail catchment area," James said. "Within fifteen kilometers, there are four thousand households that earn more than $4,000 per month, and seventy-four thousand households with more than $975 per month. That is middle income by any standard measure.* When you read the big global consulting firm reports they tell you how much wealth is in Africa or in Kenya, but that is the macro story. You would never build Two Rivers based on that. It's only when we get to the micro level like this that then the thing just grabs us."†

Revisit Assumptions: Regions Change

Aside from regional trading blocs, the most common means businesses use to segment Africa is to segment North Africa from sub-Saharan Africa, and to segment the country of South Africa from that.

At both ends of the continent, old perceptions are masking the emerging reality. As demonstrated by several CEOs succeeding there, North Africa is less distinguished from the rest of Africa than many believe. South Africa is more so.

Many Western companies and public policy analysts distinguish entirely the Arab-dominated countries of Egypt, Tunisia, Algeria, Libya, and Morocco from their neighbors to the South. In my view and the view of the business leaders I know, that's behind the curve. As mentioned above, the principal trading bloc of North Africa, the Arab Maghreb Union, does not function. As a result, trade within North Africa is very low. Participants in the Arab Spring have expressed aspirations for this to change, but they are still aspirations.

Meanwhile, trade with the rest of Africa is growing under the

---

*According to the World Bank methodology, lower middle income is $1,026–$4,035; upper middle income, $4,036–$12,475;

†To be fair, the best reports by consulting firms, and most notably McKinsey's analysis of consumer trends and urban centers, do look at primary and secondary cities. They do not, however, capture the kind of analysis that James and his partners conducted to see and act on Two Rivers.

radar. Intra-Africa trade statistics are notoriously difficult to track.*
However, business leaders succeeding in North Africa report that
they are increasingly looking to West and sub-Saharan Africa for
growth.

The new pattern is rooted in ancient ones. Mohamed El Kettani is
the CEO of Attijariwafa Bank, the largest bank in North Africa, and
rated the best bank in the region in 2010 by *African Banker* magazine. Mohamed is bespectacled, soft spoken, and avuncular. It's a
demeanor that has probably been helpful as Attijariwafa has conducted a march of acquisition over the last decade. Under Mohamed's
leadership, that march led south. The bank's predecessor (Banque
Commerciale du Maroc) merged with Wafa, its largest domestic com-
petitor, and then acquired banks in Tunisia, Senegal, Mauritania,
Mali, and Togo. In recent history, the growth opportunities for
Moroccan companies lay north, in Europe. Mohamed describes how
old bonds of culture and commerce led him to consider Africa the
better opportunity:

> With the completion of our merger with Wafa Bank in 2003, we
> were for the first time strong enough to consider international
> expansion, and we set about creating a strategic plan. Shortly
> before our merger, our king† went on three tours of Africa, and
> he was very well received. This was an important political sig-
> nal that government on both sides would be receptive to Moroc-
> can companies growing in Southern Africa. We developed our
> strategic plan very conscious of Morocco's historical role as a
> crossroad between Northern Africa and Southern Africa. When

---

*One World Bank expert with unrivaled visibility on these figures estimates
that "something between 50 percent and 100 percent of intra-African trade
does not show up in the trade data."

†Mohammad VI, the current Moroccan king. He ascended the throne in 1999.

Islam grew in Africa it went south through Morocco, so there's a cultural proximity with the Western African countries that are Islamic. Many African Muslims talk of the "Little Haj," not to Mecca, but to Fez. It emanates from the saint who's buried there. It is a holy journey for the Tijani,* which is a very large group in Western Africa. These were some of the key drivers— proximity, commercial flows, and cultural links—that the strategic plan built on.

That history is reflected in Mohamed's personal life. I asked him if when he was young, growing up in Morocco, he had thought of himself as an African. "Yes, always," he said, smiling. "My family has always told me about sub-Saharan Africa. In the early 1900s, part of the family went south to Senegal and Cote d'Ivoire and they did business there for forty years and built up wealth and then returned to Morocco. My wife's parents also spent many years in Mali and Cote D'Ivoire, trading. My mother-in-law, who is eighty-five, speaks Wolof† to this day."

Opportunities for Southern growth are not limited to Morocco. Jalilia Mezni operates Société d'Articles Hygiéniques (SAH), a Tunisian manufacturer of diapers and feminine hygiene products with $100 million in revenue. From the establishment of SAH in 1996, Jalilia has seen in Africa the natural growth trajectory of her company. SAH's initial transborder expansion was into Libya, and the company is now looking at its first transborder manufacturing operation, in the Ivory Coast. "Africa is our future," Jalilia has said.[3] Issad

---

*The Tijani are a Sufist Muslim order living primarily in Senegal, The Gambia, Mauritania, Mali, Guinea, Northern Nigeria, and Sudan. The saint Mohamed refers to is the founder of their order, Sīdī 'Aḥmad al-Tijānī (1737–1815). He is buried in Fez.

†The Wolof are an ethnic group who live primarily in Senegal, The Gambia, and Mauritania. There are about 6.2 million Wolofs.

Ribrab, CEO of Algerian steel and agro-processing business Cevital, with U.S. $3 billion in revenue, has launched his country's most significant cross-border investment initiatives in two countries: Ivory Coast and Rwanda.[4, 5]

The integration of North and sub-Saharan Africa is uneven. Egypt, with a domestic market of $230 billion* and proximity to the Gulf states, is not as integrated with Africa as Morocco is. From Egypt, the look southward is a glance by the young. Lamiaa Soliman expresses that aspiration. Lamiaa is an Egyptian currently attending Harvard Business School, after a successful early career with EFG Hermes, one of the Arab world's top investment banks. She describes her peer group's drive to connect with the rest of Africa as an outgrowth of a larger reinvention of their society:

Personally, I would say that there is a wide disconnect today between my country and the rest of Africa. That's the biggest reason why I wanted to join the Africa Business Club. In Egypt only now is there starting to be this discussion about, "Well, we should be engaging with other African countries." You're seeing it not with the largest companies, but with medium-sized companies and the upcoming generation in Egypt. It's related to a rhetoric coming out after the Arab Spring of wanting a new way of doing business. People are saying, "Why should we be waiting for government policies to set everything into place? We should be venturing south."

There continue to be significant cultural and ethnic differences between North Africa and its sub-Saharan neighbors. Notwithstanding, there are compelling commercial opportunities to be found as

---

* As of 2011

the successful firms in North Africa integrate with the growth of the rest of Africa.

South Africa is another matter. Many global companies anticipate that the best way to enter the African market is through South Africa. I find few Africans outside of South Africa who share that view.

There are both commercial and political reasons to consider South Africa as distinct from the rest of Africa. From a commercial perspective, the South African economy is larger and more developed than any other on the continent. This dimension alone is reason to perceive it as distinct.

That is how SABMiller runs its continental activity, with a South Africa business unit and a distinct Africa business unit that guides the rest of the continent. SABMiller's executive chairman Graham Mackay explained why:

At the time we started our international expansion, our South African beer business was in the top ten or so biggest beer businesses in the world. It had size, breadth, and scale techniques at hand and capital at its disposal to do things that no other businesses in Africa could muster.

The size difference is fairly fundamental, and most things flow from it. However, it's not just size. It's also the level of sophistication of the consumer, the employee base, and competition; it's the level of infrastructure as well. As a result, we have different management structures, (in South Africa and the rest of Africa) and we regard them as essentially different propositions.

Based in the commercial heart of East Africa, Vimal Shah sees it much the same way. "I don't really think of South Africa as Africa," he said. "If I say typical Africa, typical Africa is not South Africa. It has its different ways of doing business and different opportunities. There is a commonality about the rest. The rest of the sub-Saharan markets are just coming up from basic agricultural economies. The cities are half developed, and there is a huge "upside" coming. In South Africa they are much more organized, and also in South Africa you have two different, distinct groupings: the guys who have already made it there versus guys who never made it. No, this is entirely different."

Though apartheid ended in 1994, its legacy affects South Africa in many ways that distinguish it from the rest of Africa. Graham explains with an example drawn from one of SABMiller's market segments, sorghum beer:

In South Africa, many years ago, it was illegal for black people to drink "white man's" liquor, and all they were allowed to drink legally was the sorghum beer. The sorghum beer was provided in municipal beer halls, which were a local monopoly— effectively of the government. That was obviously a highly polarizing policy. Sorghum beer became, to some extent, an unwanted good, in economic terms. People traded up out of it as fast as they could. As a result of that, the sorghum beer industry in South Africa today is nowhere near as healthy, profitable, or well regarded as it is in other parts of Africa. That's kind of a political overtone that carried on.

South Africa's past is mixing with South Africa's present to create a shifting and uncertain dynamic, both for the country itself and its relationship with the rest of Africa. South Africa had been the driver of growth and innovation in Africa for more than a century. Right now, that is not the case. At the time of this writing, South Africa's growth is about 2 percent per annum, far below most of the economies of sub-Saharan Africa. It may slow further due to widespread labor unrest and a looming reexamination of not just laws but the entire social contract of post-apartheid governance.

South Africa was extraordinarily isolated from the rest of Africa for a long time, with a lingering effect on the business leaders in both South Africa and its neighbors. Born in South Africa and raised in Swaziland, Phuthuma Nhleko reflected on his first real opportunity to meet the rest of Africa, which came when he left Africa for college in the United States:

> Ohio State was interesting. It's a university town and to some extent was a bit of a cultural shock for me. I can comfortably say I met more non-South African Africans on a meaningful scale and social context for the first time outside Africa than I ever met them in Africa. I met many West and East Africans. These are not people I'd met before because South Africa was very closed. Generally speaking, South Africans didn't travel much outside the country then. Oddly enough, most South Africans, black and white, when they travelled, travelled more to the U.S., Europe, and Asia than to the rest of Africa. They knew more about places ten thousand kilometers away than places next door, with the exception of Botswana, Lesotho, and Swaziland. Those are South Africa's immediate next-door neighbors whose economies are integrally intertwined with and highly dependent on South Africa. Generally speaking, South Africans did not travel to the likes of Nigeria, Ghana, or Kenya during the apartheid period. All those were very distant places literally and metaphorically.

Phuthuma was candid about the gap that still exists between the rest of the continent and South Africa, including black South Africa. He spoke of it with the quiet reserved for sensitive topics one wants to speak about candidly:

> First of all let me say as black South Africans we accept that South Africans in many respects are quite indebted to the role

that a number of African countries played in the anti-apartheid movement and their support of black South Africans when things were really difficult and dark. Africans continent-wide were absolutely delighted to see South Africa being eventually liberated. It presented a lot of opportunities for all.

My sense is that quite a number of Africans outside of South Africa have been somewhat disappointed that South Africans have not been as open-minded and welcoming of other African countries and the people from various parts of the continent. And, in fact, in some quarters, we South Africans from time to time, have operated under certain unfortunate stereotypes that are exacerbated by the scramble for limited jobs, housing, etc. Because few of us had spent any meaningful time in the rest of Africa pre-1990, there has always been a huge degree of sheer ignorance of certain aspects and, unfortunately, ignorance cannot always be eliminated overnight: it takes time.

At times this has played itself out in the approach that certain South African companies take as they're trying to enter African markets. In certain quarters of the rest of Africa, it is seen as being a little bit dominating or even, unfairly, a mini imperialist approach. That's unfortunate, but I'm hopeful that, over time, increased exposure all around will create more wisdom on both sides, as there is huge potential and opportunity that would benefit all parties.

For SABMiller's Graham Mackay, the effect of apartheid was not just a small world, but a shrinking one over the course of his early life and career:

For anybody growing up in South Africa during the days of apartheid, we had a passing knowledge of some of the surrounding countries, because we would, very often, go there on holiday and visit game parks and the resort areas. It didn't really extend up into East Africa and Central Africa, because certainly by the time I was an adult, white South Africans were personae non grata out there. I suppose you could have traveled up there, but I didn't, and I didn't know anyone who did.

I was a bit atypical, because I was brought up in Swaziland, not in South Africa. We used to go to Mozambique a lot when I was a child. That was before the revolution, in '75 and '76. I knew Swaziland and Mozambique extremely well. I lived in what was then Rhodesia (known since 1980 as The Republic of Zimbabwe) for a while, when I was growing up, so I knew that as well. Most white South Africans were quite familiar with those territories. I suppose we regarded the accessible part of Africa's border as Northern Rhodesia, then.

That changed as apartheid tightened and we became more and more isolated. There were other events, including revolutions with a change of government, in both Mozambique and in Angola, and the Bush War in Rhodesia, all of which deepened our isolation. The isolation came to an end toward the end of the '80s, when Nelson Mandela was released and it was obvious that apartheid was crumbling.

The history of South Africa's isolation has left a disconnect between South Africa and the rest of Africa that affects how success is achieved in each. The current evolution of South African politics only heightens this distinction. Several CEOs commented that they see current struggles in the ruling African National Congress (ANC) as comparable to the paroxysms of governance the rest of the continent experienced thirty or more years ago. A South African business leader who was deeply engaged in the transition to ANC leadership and the development of the current structure said recently over drinks, "What I see is the unraveling of our national compact. We will need to make another." In this regard, South Africa is a young polity governing a mature economy.

Hopefully, South Africa will right itself quickly. Even if it does, businesses in Africa and outside of it should be aware of the distinction (and sometimes the distance) between South Africa and its neighbors, at least over the short term.

The Right Lens: A Differentiated Whole

Understanding the distinctions between Africa's many parts is critical to understanding what success means in Africa. Cognizant of these distinctions, many business leaders also pursue success in Africa with a continent-wide lens.

The most obvious reason is economies of scale. Tom Gibian first observed them when he was working in Asia, before he began work in Africa:

In Africa, you can't be a little pregnant. The Asian shipping lines and logistics firms saw this early on. Their business just didn't work if they had to give up their manifests for last-mile transport. So, once they decided they were coming to Africa, they were all in. They made sure they could transport to every major port. The same is true in my business. We found that, to build a world-class private equity business, you couldn't go small. To attract the right capital and world-class talent, you couldn't go small. You had to do the whole continent.

That logic was also compelling to Tim Solso when he was looking for the next significant growth opportunity for $18 billion engine and power generation manufacturer, Cummins, Inc. Square-jawed, mountainous, and rugged, Tim was born in the coastal state of Oregon, but is very much a product of the American Midwest. After attending DePauw University in Greencastle, Indiana, he earned a Harvard MBA, then returned to Indiana with Cummins, which is based in Columbus, Indiana. Tim rose to the top at Cummins and became CEO and chairman in 2000. "In my last five years with the company," he said, "I wanted to find the next growth area for Cummins, one that the company ten years from now could benefit from."

After some intense investigation, Tim determined that growth area was Africa. It was during that time that I met Tim, and together we met some two dozen CEOs from all corners of the continent (Tim was explicit that he wanted to look at the whole continent). Years later, I asked him why he did not focus on a couple of big national markets or one regional market. "Never an option for me," he said, in a clipped tone that is all about efficiency. "My goal was to move the needle for Cummins. It had to make sense from that perspective." Like ECP's Tom Gibian, he found that a continental vision helped to attract the talent Cummins needed to succeed. "The guy I asked to lead us in Africa is a phenomenally capable talent in our organization, and was previously leading distribution in Asia. For him to come and attract the team he wanted, the opportunity had to be big: all Africa."

While economies of scale are compelling, much of that benefit could be realized at the regional level. Operating in the 140-million-person market of the East African Community or the 380-million-person market of COMESA would probably yield the economy of scale necessary to compete, while gaining the advantage of market focus.*

Ultimately, the best reason to approach Africa as a whole is because that is increasingly how Africans see it. Mo Ibrahim saw the economies of scale that appealed to Tom at ECP and Tim at Cummins, but also sees much more. "There is something common about the

---

*Population figures are based on July 2012 estimates from the CIA World Factbook

African people," Mo told me over dinner. "While politically there are fifty-four countries, there is some form of an African identity."

"I don't think our company would have been a success unless it became an all-African business," Mo said. "Whenever I meet somebody else in the room from Africa, they will come to me as an African. Not as Mo Ibrahim, not for what I've done, but because they look at you as an African, and they'll say or feel 'Oh, hi, brother.' There is this something on an emotional level that binds us. It allowed Celtel to create a brand across the region."

Today, African identity is a critical feature of politics, trade, and branding. Bharat Thakrar makes his living understanding branding across Africa. His views on African identity are captured in how he describes an exceptional event that resonated broadly across the continent:

Brand aspiration in Africa is different than in the U.S. or Europe. It's being proud of who I am, proud of being African. It's a sense that it's our time now. The best example was during the last football World Cup. The last African team standing was Ghana and the whole continent was supporting Ghana. Scangroup had just set up a business there and in our internal messaging system everyone was sending messages to our Ghanaian employees from everywhere in the continent, "We are with you." Suddenly every Ghanaian got support from every African that he knew on the continent. It was so emotional for every African that Ghana win. You will not find that in a European country, nor in North or South America, for that matter.

At Dalberg, about 50 percent of the global staff are in Africa. We experienced exactly the same phenomenon.

ECP founder Tom Gibian, who first went to Africa after completing his MBA at Wharton, has observed the change in African identity over time. "If you went to Africans fifteen or twenty years ago," he told me, "they would have said 'I am from Gabon or I am an Ijaw,' and that was the limit of their ambition. That was two generations of African business leaders ago. They relied on political relationships to secure advantage in the market. That really was something you could do at the national level, but only at that level. That's not the ambition or the value proposition of African business leaders today. They base it on competitiveness, which can cross boundaries. If you go to business schools now and ask any African students what their ambition is, if they're going back home,* it's for all of Africa."

Ken Njoroge embodies the competitive and continental ambition Tom describes. Ken is the CEO of Cellulant, a Nairobi-based developer of mobile commerce solutions for banks, airlines, merchants, and governments. Ken and his partner started the company with a desk, a whiteboard, and a credit card. Ken still sits at the same desk. The whiteboard is wearing through in places but it's still in service next to the desk. Today, Cellulant operates in eight countries and is among Africa's leaders in mobile payment solutions. KPMG called it the top mid-sized company in Kenya.

Ken's start in life was tough. "My dad wasn't around from an early age, and my mother was strict, so we worked." He sees growing up poor as an asset. "When we were in school we had no books, so my mom said that just meant that my brother and I had to be able to listen to the teacher give the lesson, and understand it the first time. I still have good recall because of it."

Cellulant is based in a country of 42 million people, and operates in the East African Community, a market of about 140 million. For Ken, that's too small. He explains:

---

* In a recent survey conducted by private equity firm Jacana Partners, 70 percent of Africans in global business schools are planning to return to Africa. See http://bit.ly/VAYFri for details.

From the outset, I wanted to build a world-class business, and it became clear to me that if you want to build a world-class business in Africa you need to address a market that's larger than your borders. Early in my career, I worked with MTN. I could see it was a world-class company that went right across Africa. That really caught my attention. It was great for me to see in real time a business that started from a humble beginning and then went out across the continent and achieved a level of respectability and brand presence and brand recognition. Those were very formative in shaping the theater of my ambition.

That ambition can now be realized, in part because of the advancement in connectivity described in chapter 2. "Because of the availability of data and communication around Africa," Ken says, "we talk about our presence in Ghana and Nigeria in almost casual terms." It wasn't always the case, Ken pointed out, laughing. "You know, when I talk with some of the older generation and I tell them we have an operation in Nigeria. They say, 'What, in Nigeria? How do you manage to do business?' I say, 'Look, the amount of effort it takes to get into Nigeria is the same amount of effort it takes to get into Rwanda or to get into Uganda, but the payoff is not the same. It's far higher.'"*

African identity is driven by many factors. One that's little discussed but particularly relevant for retail and consumer brands is the legacy of failed institutions at the national level. In the absence of national parties and governments that deliver results, consumers find brands that deliver for them, even across national boundaries. Bharat Thakrar explains:

---

* Nigeria has a population of 162 million and is the first- or second-largest economy in Africa.

People feel they have been deprived. First they were deprived or let down by the colonials. Then they feel they were let down by their own political group or political class who took power with promises to bring schools, education, hospitals, and then ate the money themselves. Then an opposition group came to power with the same result, and people became very cynical about the political class. Now they feel these guys are just a waste of time. That created a vacuum, where these big Pan-African brands came in and started playing the roles that parties and governments were not playing to the same extent, and affinity started going more toward the brand rather than the party or what have you.

In this particular regard, it may be easier for companies and brands to gain adherents across borders in Africa than in other parts of the world, where the competition for affinity is stronger. Bharat concluded with an observation that may be more whimsical than telling, but it sticks with me: "Very few Africans can trace the outline of their country," he said, pulling out a piece of paper and pencil. He began to outline, looking up at me, "but we all know what Africa looks like." He handed me a perfectly rendered outline of Africa.

There is no more visible corporate expression of a whole Africa than the mobile phone giant MTN, which operates in nineteen African countries. The man who helped build that empire, Phuthuma Nhleko, is mentioned as a model by many of the other business leaders in this book. Fifty-three years old, Phuthuma is erudite, relaxed, and hip. He traces his consciousness of a whole Africa to the writings of African intellectuals Kwame Nkrumah, Robert Sobukwe, and Stephen Biko. He also credits his student days in the United States, specifically to studying at Ohio State and at Atlanta University, the oldest of America's historically black colleges:

Becoming Africa

When I think back to my early twenties, Atlanta University was the crucible of a worldview that looked at life differently. The ethos of the institution was that history education should not be focused only on the period that commences AD 01, that you need to go back to 4000 BC or longer. If you go back to 4000–5000 BC you go back to the older civilizations like Egypt, and you are enlightened about other states and peoples and the depth of civilization around Egypt. If I were minister of education in Africa for a day, I would legislate a set of books of the likes of Cheikh Anta Diop's *The African Origin of Civilization*. At the very least, even if one is at variance with his theory, it puts a very different perspective on one's worldview and what established media would have developing Africa believe as a reflection of its own image and position in the world.

It takes away the damaging, incorrect, and highly peddled notion that African people just "emerged" yesterday and contributed nothing. Because that is a mere sliver of purposefully selective recent history that is uneducated and makes the misinformer feel a sense of subliminal superiority. You need to go far back. The same simplification and ignorance of Chinese history is promoted in today's mass media. They give the impression that China has just arrived. Well, China has arrived before; this is just the second or third time, right? I think those are very important perspectives that shape how young Africans begin to see themselves. For me as a twenty-year-old, it started shaping my mind about Africa, where it has been, what it could be, where it fits in the world and where it needs to go.

The emergence of business leaders like Phuthuma, Mo, and Ken is manifesting in increased African investment in Africa, a prerequisite of continental growth. That change can be seen in figure 3–5.

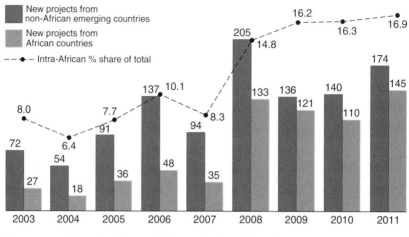

Figure 3–5: Growth of intra-African foreign direct investment

Source: Ernst & Young. *Africa by the Numbers.* 2012. By permission.

According to Ernst & Young, the number of investments in Africa by Africa climbed fourfold from 2007 to 2011. In the same period, intra-African investments as a share of the total number of investments in Africa doubled, from 8.3 percent to 16.9 percent,[6] an early indication of Africa's growing belief in itself.

As African business steps on the world stage, talented African managers are returning home and emerging domestically. They are expressing greater faith in their opportunities and helping to define an African identity. Like leaders of emerging continents before them, they are also defining an approach to capitalism appropriate to their time and place.

CHAPTER 4

Africapitalism

You can't ignore the markets where there is nothing. Those are the markets that buy everything.
Dr. Chris Kirubi, Chairman, International House Limited

Africa needs everything, and success in Africa comes from filling that need. That seems a straightforward equation, but it has eluded many companies that have operated in Africa, including many African companies. James Mworia recalls an experience that captures the phenomenon well. When this story took place, James had already been to university, become a CPA, and was working full time at Centum:

I remember when I was an employee of Centum in 2001, I got a letter from my bank, Standard Chartered Bank. They said, "Based on your balance and the activity in your account, you're not qualified to be an account holder in this bank. You have so many days to collect your money," and they closed my account. That's not a long time ago. Individuals like me who were working for a listed company could not even afford to be banked. What happens to everybody else?

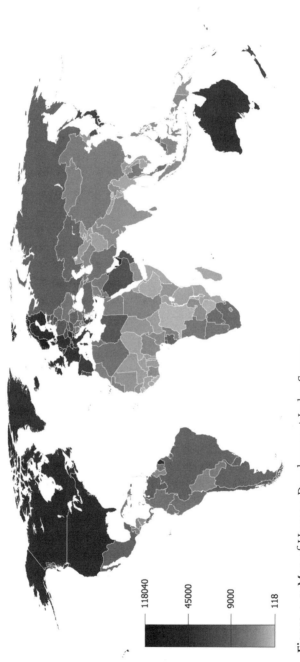

Figure 4–1: Map of Human Development Index Scores

Source: UN Development Program, provided to Wikimedia December 18, 2011.

In late 2012 I met the CEO of a U.S.-based global consumer and investment bank that was reported to have significant plans for expansion in Africa. "Yes, we're growing our presence in Africa," the banking CEO confirmed. He summarized the company's plans to service global corporate clients as they expanded across the continent. I asked him if he planned to bank anyone else while in Africa. He looked at me quizzically. "Like who?" he asked.

Africa can look like a place where only the few can buy anything. The World Bank's calculation of gross domestic product per capita rates Africa the lowest of any region in the world. Figure 4–1 shows Africa's relative place in the human development index (HDI), a compilation of income, health, education, and other socioeconomic metrics.

Africa needs everything. What an opportunity.

Need is not the same thing as the inability to pay. Africa's consumer sector is growing rapidly. While natural resources contributed about a third to Africa's growth in the decade from 2000 to 2010, consumer-facing and partially consumer-facing industries contributed 45 percent of that growth, according to a 2012 McKinsey & Company report, *The Rise of the African Consumer.** The authors predict that more than half of African households will have discretionary income by 2020, which is an increase from 85 million today to 130 million. Along with that, they project consumer industries (including retail/wholesale, retail banking, telecom, and tourism) will grow by more than $400 billion by 2020. That forecasted increase is more

---

*The McKinsey report is based on a survey of thirteen thousand consumers from fifteen cities in ten countries in 2011 and 2012, with a focus on the largest African cities.

than half of the total projection for all business revenue growth over the period.[2]

Much of the growth in Africa's wealth is hidden. This is true both statistically and literally. Statistically, the World Bank's GDP figures are based on the formal economy only, meaning income reported to the government. The size of the informal economy is unknown, but informal work is estimated to represent almost 80 percent of nonagricultural employment, more than 60 percent of urban employment, and over 90 percent of new jobs in Africa through the mid 2000s.[3] In his influential study, financed by the World Bank's Doing Business project, Friedrich Schneider found that the informal economy represented on average over 42 percent of GNP in the early 2000s.[4] Though urbanization and formalization have probably decreased the informal sector's share somewhat, the result is that official GDP figures consistently understate the purchasing power in African villages and cities. As a cautionary tale on relying on these figures, African investor Miles Morland points out that just an adjustment in how the economy is measured caused Ghana's reported GDP to jump by 70 percent in one year.[5]

Equity Bank CEO James Mwangi has a more granular view of informal spending in Africa's villages and cities. The sixth of seven children raised by a widow, James grew up poor in rural Kenya. Though his family insisted on schooling, he also sold fruits and hauled charcoal for pay as a child. It was his first exposure to the retail customers operating at the margins of the formal economy. It is on the strength of those customers that James has built Equity Bank, the largest in East Africa. Today Equity has 7.8 million accounts and a market capitalization of over $1.3 billion. In 2012, James was named Africa's businessperson of the year by *Forbes*.

James relates the success of Equity to those early lessons hauling coal to customers. "I saw that they have money, but they need it right away, and they keep it nearby," he told me recently. "That money was hidden in mattresses before it was with Equity."

One reason James's competitors failed to serve the low-income customer is because they viewed that customer as an unacceptable credit risk. In fact, Equity Bank's nonperforming loan (NPL) rate was an industry-beating 3.0 percent in the third quarter of 2012.[6] That same false perception of credit risk is evident for Africa as a whole. According to a 2012 report to the G20 by the consulting firm Roland Berger, the cost of capital in Africa assumes a rate of nonperforming loans of 15 percent, when it is actually 8 percent. According to the G20 report, this misperception of risk alone means excess costs of up to $9 billion annually.[7]

GE finds opportunities in Africa where others routinely misperceive risk. "There's perceived risk here," Jay Ireland explained, "but if we think about credit defaults and bankruptcies, where have we seen more of that in the last eight years? The U.S. and Europe, or Africa? There's no leverage here, we're facing no risk from that. Every project is backed by sovereign credit guarantee and a letter of credit. Also, not paying your creditors in Africa means going out of business. American Airlines went into bankruptcy, but still flies. That's not an option for most companies in Africa, so they pay. Some Westerners tend not to see that."

Business leaders who succeed in Africa have observed need and recognized it as an opportunity to expand, rather than shrink, their addressable market. That dynamic is not limited to low-income or "base of the pyramid" customers. Chris Kirubi's businesses sell to rich and poor alike. One of his more recent ventures is in biometric identification, a scan of your thumb or eye to confirm identity. Once the purview of James Bond movies, biometrics are an occasional feature of developed-country economies. They meet a pressing and widespread challenge in frontier markets like Africa's, where companies want to extend food and health-care benefits to their workers without risking a mass expansion of informal beneficiaries. Chris explains:

We're moving directly to biometrics so that we skip over photo ID cards, which somebody gives to his cousin to go to the clinic. We are rolling it out across the whole of Kenya, as well as Uganda. The next will be Rwanda and Tanzania. Some of our corporate customers have saved as much as 40 percent of their medical bills the past year. Now, we're extending the service to track attendance at work so you don't give your friend your card to punch you in or out. We're extending it to corporate canteens where employees eat so that no Tom, Dick, and Harry can walk in where you're serving.

Sunny Verghese was not raised in Africa, but his decades of experience there let him see the current opportunity in meeting Africa's needs. Sunny is the founding CEO of Olam, a $14 billion global agribusiness with a market capitalization of U.S. $3 billion. He was raised in India and trained among that country's first generation of globally competitive business leaders, attending India's prestigious Indian Institute of Management (IIM) in the early 1980s. After a four-year stint with Unilever's Indian subsidiary, Sunny was asked by the Kewalram Chanrai (KC) Group to manage its agribusiness affairs in Africa. "While I was at business school, Africa was not much mentioned," Sunny recalls. "When I first went to Africa, it was a complete eye-opener for me. The KC Group was already doing good business there, and I could see it getting much better as governments relaxed their hold on commodities and on farmers."

Sunny positioned the newly formed Olam to serve the role that had previously been managed (and often mismanaged) by government procurement boards. The company has since expanded its African businesses dramatically. Today Olam's operations in eighteen African countries extend from farming to branded consumer foods.

Sunny is sharp, to the point, and extremely detail oriented across geographies and commodities. He will tell you the prevailing wage rate in Colombia, the going price for coffee in Tanzania, and the average inflation rate across Africa in a single breath. In Africa, Sunny sees continued opportunity to supply global agribusiness needs. However, he also sees opportunity in Africa's rising demand:

> Given our portfolio of products, Africa is very important as a source of origin, but Africa is also very important from a market point of view. For example, Africa has the potential to become self-sufficient in rice. Out of the world's thirty million to fifty million tons of rice that is traded, Africa imports about nine million tons of that. So almost a third of the world's rice trade goes into Africa. I believe that Africa does not have to spend a single dollar of foreign exchange to import its rice. It can grow all its rice and be self-sufficient. Africa also imports almost all of its wheat, nearly thirty million tons, because we've not harnessed Africa's potential so far. Olam has supplied those products into Africa in the past, but today, we turned towards growing them in Africa for Africa.
>
> Then there is the opportunity to provide Africa with processed food. Most of the multinational branded companies dismiss Africa as a niche market, and a very difficult market in which to execute. Most of the products that they sell in Africa are not based on real market or consumer insight, and they're not targeted and adapted to African tastes or African price points. We see a huge opportunity to tailor-make consumer food products in Africa with low unit price, high quality, and value-for-money products that are based on solid consumer insights and research about African consumer taste and how it is developing.

Seeing the opportunity in need drives success in Africa even for companies that are not selling to Africans. I recently worked with a mining company producing in West Africa entirely for export to Asia.

The company had a register of several hundred social and economic risks associated with its operation, and sought an overarching architecture to manage them. Ultimately, the company found the entire register had its roots in a single meta-challenge: *We run a multi-billion dollar project in a region where people earn $100 a year. How do we convert that gap into opportunities, now and for the next hundred years?*

Perceiving the opportunities in bridging that gap, rather than just the risks, changed the dynamic of how the company manages not only community affairs, but its entire supply, production, and transit operation.

Success Lies in Bridging Gaps

Many needs in Africa go unmet not because the solution doesn't exist or can't be afforded. Rather, they go unmet because of bridgeable gaps: gaps between buyers and sellers; between governments and their constituents; and between companies and their communities. Business leaders succeeding in Africa close those gaps.

One of the most valuable gaps to close is the literal one, distance. Africa is a vast continent that is sparsely populated with people, infrastructure, and services. GE is adapting its product line to the realities of distance.

"We've developed V-scan, which is a handheld ultrasound," Jay Ireland explained as an example. "We're working with nurse-midwives to help them understand the device and transmit the information back to the clinic via mobile coverage. The clinic and nurse-midwife can then consult and triage which mothers could deliver in a local birthing center and who should go to a more advanced facility. Now we're adding a rugged little solar panel on the V-Scan so it can be charged anywhere."

GE has also had commercial success closing the gap of distance by selling a battery adapted to power African mobile phone towers. "In developed markets you just plug the tower into the grid," Jay said. "Africa's distances from the grid are a lot greater, so they've used diesel to power the towers. We adapted this battery from our locomotive division to do the same job. It cuts the tower's use of diesel by 40 percent."

There may be no sector in which distance has proven a more profitable gap to close than in banking. In Equity Bank's early years under James Mwangi's leadership, the company would drive armored trucks out to villages and set them up as mobile banks. More recently, Equity has developed an agency model for banking in which the customer-facing functions of the bank are handled by a local shop owner. James describes some of the impact on the customer, and on Equity Bank:

> The agency is a clear symbol of our understanding the customer. This customer needs his money nearby because his life is unplanned. The cost of financial services is not the principal hindrance to this customer—the physical distance to the branches is. It's the cost of surmounting that barrier. It's the amount of time that one would take to go to where the bank is. It's the amount of money that one would pay on public transport. We've been in existence for twenty-six years. The number of transactions done by branch banking in those twenty-six years has now been surpassed by the transactions done by the agents in just two years.

Equity uses agency banking to help close another gap: the gap between traditional and modern. "All the people of Equity, the people developing and delivering our product, are educated and modern," James said. "A bank, itself, is modern. Our customer is largely traditional. For the interface with our customer to be smooth, it must be accommodating. It must show compassion." James describes how the agency model does that:

The rural customer found the bank very sophisticated. He was being intimidated by marble, granite, and glass cubicles. When he goes to the shop, he's very familiar with the shopkeeper and the language of the shopkeeper. The bank is demystified. Savings is explained in a local language and context. Instead of calling it a bank, the shopkeeper says, "This is your granary of money." They have granaries where they keep their maize and seed. I would never have made my way to how they introduce a bank as a granary. You can see that the shopkeeper demystifies the code, turning the banking language into the layman's language.

The gap between traditional and formal economy is one that's bridged profitably in many sectors. Just as Equity Bank helps people bring their money out of the mattress, SABMiller finds a market among Africans whose previous option was a satisfying but irregular and unstable home brew. Graham Mackay explains how his company meets that consumer on the first rung of the commercial beer market:

The bottom of the market in our game is informal alcohol, mostly home-brew. Nobody really knows for sure, but around 50 percent of all the alcohol consumed in Africa is informal, untaxed, and effectively home-brewed beer made from sorghum or other grains.* Today, we've become the biggest commercial players in sorghum beer in Africa. Most sorghum beer is sold still fermenting. It's alive and sold in containers that are vented to allow the pressure to escape. You sell it up until about five days,

---

* Beer enthusiasts around the world, including me, love home brew. When 50 percent of alcohol consumed in a country is outside the formal sector, it presents social, health, and fiscal challenges.

after which it starts to go off. It has a very, very short shelf life. We have recently introduced sorghum beer at a slightly higher price point, but with an arrested fermentation so it's shelf-stable. We have also introduced other hybrid products, lager-type beers made with a high proportion of sorghum and cassava. Those are also attractive to lower-income-level consumers.

Graham reflected on low-income consumers and a relationship to the product that changes as the consumer earns more. "There's a saying in business that a poor consumer doesn't regard himself as poor," he said. "He regards himself as only temporarily strapped for funds. Our hope is that he stays with us on a chain up to our premium products."

Graham's foresight in closing gaps with the African consumer garners praise from Neville Isdell, who led Coca-Cola as chairman and CEO. Neville recalled that "Graham was criticized for the acquisitions he was making in Africa. People said there was no money there. Look at the business he's built. He showed that if that demographic includes a whole lot of poor people, maybe you're not going to sell too many Ferraris, but you can serve them profitably wherever they are in their level of consumer development."

Sometimes the gap between provider and recipient is so big the product never even arrives. For years, the government of Nigeria provided up to $250 million in annual subsidies to some twenty million farmers to buy fertilizer. Ninety percent of the subsidy did not arrive, lost to a combination of mismanagement and misappropriation by various middlemen.

Ken Njoroge's Cellulant was hired to close the gap between the subsidy and those twenty million farmers intended to receive it. Together with Cellulant cofounder Bolaji Akinboro, Ken had won a contract to develop a mobile payments solution that would put the fertilizer subsidy directly in the hands of the farmers (we'll talk more about how that contract was won in chapter 6).

Working with the Nigerian Ministry of Agriculture, Cellulant developed a solution in which an accredited farmer receives a PIN sent to his phone, which carries with it a credit for the full subsidy. The recipient takes the PIN to any accredited agro distributor and can redeem its full value. Because proper fertilization has a multiplying effect on crop yields, the effect on farmer income is dramatic. By ensuring the full subsidy gets to the farmer, the system is expected to boost the average farmer's income from $700 to $1,800 over three to four seasons.[8]

Ken described both the project's impact and the implications for future revenue for the farmer and for Cellulant. "By creating this structure we have given farmers a mobile wallet and begun them on the path of financial inclusion," Ken explained. "Their transaction history is there. They have sufficient data about what they're growing, what they buy, etc. All that data helps the farmer plan, and will help a bank have confidence to lend." It also creates for Cellulant a unique database with consumer insights on Africa's most populous country. Ken is not shy about his ambitions for the e-wallet. "Over the last year, we've shifted government policy on the disbursement of fertilizer subsidies. There is no question that this is going to be the mechanism through which subsidy is given for every other thing in Nigeria in the next few years."

Closing the gap to customers previously neglected by the market has very real benefits in terms of brand loyalty. What a brand or company can mean is transformed. Scangroup CEO Bharat Thakrar explained that "if you stop a European and ask him the brand that means the most to him he will tell you Apple, BMW, or Mercedes. For most consumers in Africa, it will be their cell phone operator."

It is a stark contrast. Do you know many people in the United

States or Europe who love their cell phone company? Everyone I know hates their cell phone company.

"The relationship is very simple," Bharat continued. "If you look at a mobile phone, they're using that to send money, they're using that to communicate as never before. They have a lot closer connection with the mobile companies because mobile companies are doing a lot more for them."

Operating amidst need does not mean closing gaps only on the demand side. Successful business leaders in Africa also close gaps between their companies and suppliers. Aidan Heavey captures Tullow's perspective after thirty years in Africa:

> We take the view that where we find oil we can't be just about producing oil. We have to make sure that the oil industry becomes a local industry, that the services that are supplied to us and others come from local companies or partnerships between local companies and foreign companies. Ghana is a great example. We set up a division to maximize the services we're supplied by local companies, and to make sure that if international entities come in to serve us, they co-venture with local companies and build up the expertise locally. That way you can actually transform a whole economy.

In 2011 Tullow procured $120 million in goods and services locally in Ghana and Uganda, its two largest operations in Africa. As important, the company formally assesses the bids of its major global suppliers on the basis of their plans to build capabilities among Ghanaian firms. Tullow also invests in building those capabilities itself.

The global natural resource sector has not always covered itself in glory when it comes to building African economies. Today, however, these elements of national supplier development are becoming the norm among the oil, gas, and mining companies active in frontier markets, including Africa. Reporting of local supplier data still lags behind financial or health and safety reporting (which is strong in these sectors), but rising expectations will drive them to improvement in the future.

For Main One's Funke Opeke, closing the gap with suppliers means catalyzing the digital content that she can deliver through her cable. She sees the development of those digital content suppliers as part of a broader effort to create an ecosystem of broadband applications that will drive her business:

We are the advocate for the growth of the Internet ecosystem in our countries. That means promoting local content and hosting and distribution of local content. We actively seek out Nigerian content writers to get them onto our network, because we think the more relevant local content we have, the more the user base grows and the higher the utilization we're likely to experience. We're also now looking at other value-added services that support the ecosystem. We're opening the first major data centers in Nigeria, because they don't exist today, and they make it more affordable for large-scale systems to be deployed here. If you have a facility that can offer data storage for a good price, then people don't have to build their own, and we can stimulate a lot of content.

SABMiller also takes on leadership of a business ecosystem to close gaps between themselves, their suppliers, and government. It's a model that engages SABMiller in roles it doesn't play elsewhere, including that of a trade association. Graham Mackay explains:

The emerging markets are different in the sense that actions of individual companies are much higher profile and are proportionately more powerful. So we can change the course of the economy in Uganda or Zambia to an extent that we can't possibly do in the U.K. or the U.S. Not only that, but the businesses we try to catalyze, like distribution and input farming, all of those exist already in the first world, and have their own representation with government.

To give you one example, we want to help a sorghum or barley farming sector or commercial cassava farming sector to develop. We not only have to do it ourselves, but then represent it to government, so that it gets a fair shake, gets the right resources allocated to it, and doesn't get taxed out of existence. In the U.S., the barley farming business has its own representation in Washington. The same is even more true of downstream distribution, because you have the wholesale associations. They're extremely powerful, and they paddle their own canoe. In the markets of Africa, we are the ones who have to be paddling.

The supply base in Africa is often fragmented, leading successful companies of all sizes to adapt their sourcing model without sacrificing their total cost of ownership. Both global agribusiness Olam and regional agribusiness Bidco engage in direct transactions with armies of small growers surrounding their plantations. Olam CEO Sunny Verghese explains that this is part of the commercial farming model of the future in Africa, as in other frontier markets:

I believe we will see two systems for commercial agriculture in the future. One is the large mechanized model in use today in North America, South America, and Australia. But if you look at India, China, or Africa, where agriculture contributes a big chunk of their GDP, it is not possible for the government to anticipate large-scale farming in the near term because so many people make their living off the land.

Our model in these places is a nucleus plantation where we do farming at world-class standards and get very high productivity.

Around our nucleus farm, we maintain large outgrower programs. We provide all the agriculture input, including feeds, fertilizer, chemicals, pest control systems, and advice on planting density, etc. Just in that work, we were able to move rice farmers in Nigeria from one and a half tons to about three and a half or four tons per hectare. In our own plantation, we are getting about seven and a half tons. That is one crop and we are hoping, through better irrigation management, to get the farmers to produce two and a half crops a year. There is a green revolution still to happen in Africa that will transform productivity under the small holder farming system.

Strictly Business

There may be no more important gap to close than between company and community. I am sometimes reluctant to emphasize corporate social responsibility (CSR) and social investment when writing or speaking about Africa, out of concern that the entire continent will be immediately tagged as a charity case, and not really about business. Scangroup's Bharat Thakrar expresses well the right context for social investments and closing the gap with communities in Africa:

Sales are driven and maintained in Africa by delivering public goods because often nobody else is doing it, because the government is not doing it. I was in one little village the other day and there was a concert being organized by one of the telco companies. The event was thoroughly branded: "We are bringing you this concert here, we are bringing you entertainment on a Saturday afternoon." There is no public entertainment in that little village, no space to put it on or funding for the players.

This company goes in, sets up a rig, and starts giving you some entertainment? You're bound to find some relationship with the company because they're doing that and nobody else is. When there is no water and a company comes and builds water pumps, you're bound to feel that. When there's a gap and you fill that gap, people remember. We see that when we go out to measure brands. It affects brand loyalty scores.

Olam sees social investment as necessary to securing its assets. Sunny Verghese is unambiguous (and unsentimental) in describing the realities of success in a frontier market:

For us, the big lesson that we have learned is that when you go into developing economies, it is always very easy to get a license from the government to operate in those markets, but it's far tougher to get a license from the communities to operate. If you think that, because the government has given you a license, you can really go and operate in these places, you're totally mistaken. Unless the communities where you're operating believe that you're going to be adding value to them, your potential to work in those countries is going to be severely limited. You might be there for two, three, four years, but you will be evicted eventually because the communities where you're operating do not see the value. From a shareholder point of view, it makes so much sense because investing in farming, you need a long-term renewing asset. That is very valuable for my shareholders, but to get that, I need the community to see that I'm adding value, creating jobs, improving their livelihood, enhancing their income.

Sunny points out it's not charity. Charity gets him in trouble with shareholders:

Shareholders get upset when you tell them that you want to devote X percent of your income for charitable donations. They will tell you that, "If you have surplus money, give it back to me in the form of dividends. My mother died of cancer and I'm more partial to cancer research." But when you tell your shareholders that you're engaging in a variety of developmental initiatives which have some reciprocal value for the company, there are no questions asked. The whole ecosystem is making your business model more sustainable and the shareholders are happy about that. The shareholder will invest when he sees the value for it, but he gets upset when you allocate some capital to sponsor an art exhibition or something to do with sports or something that is not related to your business.

Engagement in public goods can go too far. In the United States and England, the image of the company town is not a good one, and rightly so. Companies closing the gap with African communities struggle to get the balance right between their role and governments' (roles that shift over time, and that are different in different locations). Aidan Heavey describes some of Tullow's errors and the principles he draws from them:

When we started off, first in Senegal and then in Uganda, we were getting involved so heavily in the community we actually took over a lot of the responsibilities of government. We were basically seen as the supplier of schools and hospitals. We also built all the roads and all the infrastructure. Where you get heavily involved, you do become the government in some people's views. You have to try and stop that. That's where it's helpful to be working with the government to make sure that these projects are seen as government-led. You may have helped fund them, but they have to be seen as government projects.

Of course, the answer goes beyond appearances to substance. The best cases I have seen of large-scale social investments have the following components: they are driven by demands in the community, not dreamed up in an office; they have a proven return on investment to the company (and one should not be shy about that—most of the governments and communities I've worked with expect it); and most social investments should have an exit strategy in which a government or local NGO is enabled to take over responsibility for the project. Those are pretty bare-bones principles, and nearly every large company would say that's what they are doing. If you conduct field visits and audits of the social investments in Africa, however, you will find only the most successful companies are operating that way.

In Africa, as in most frontier markets, operating profitably and addressing the needs in the surrounding environment is essentially the same challenge. It is not a matter of parallel value or shared value, nor does it have to be measured on a double or triple bottom line. Meeting needs in Africa delivers to a long-term single bottom line.*

Tony Elumelu captures this concept in a turn of phrase he coined that lends its name to this chapter. *Africapitalism*, as Tony defines it, is "an economic philosophy that embodies the private sector's commitment to the economic transformation of Africa through long-term investments that create both economic prosperity and social wealth." Most of the investments discussed in *Success in Africa* exhibit these characteristics. They have origins outside of any social

---

*NYU economist Dan Altman and I have written more on the merits of a long-term single bottom line approach. For a summary, please see *Stamford Social Innovation Review*, June 24, 2011.

mission, but are delivering social wealth because that is what works in Africa.

That reality is reflected in the way CEOs spend their time in Africa. In 2011 PricewaterhouseCoopers conducted a survey of CEOs around the world, asking about the role they saw for themselves in the coming year. African CEOs saw their role in much the same ways as CEOs elsewhere, with one area of divergence. Fully 75 percent of African CEOs planned an increased corporate commitment to poverty reduction. Globally that figure was 42 percent.[9]

Delivering what Tony Elumelu describes as social wealth, whether through product, supply chain, or social investment, insulates companies from a host of risks and opens opportunities in other parts of the world. Tullow has experienced this as it expanded across the continent. Aidan Heavey explains:

If you're looking at investing in a big asset in a country, the biggest issue that you have is political risk. Political risk involves a huge number of issues. It's taxation, it's taking away of your assets, it's whatever. Each of those risks is mitigated by the posture we've taken, because what you become is a very important citizen in that country. I think that is a good place to be. If you're a big employer, if you have a lot of local companies working for you and you're well respected as a company, you're in a lot better place than somebody who isn't.

Ken Njoroge's Cellulant is clearly delivering social wealth through its work in Nigerian fertilizer, and in easing mobile payments across east Africa. It is equally true that Cellulant is rewarded profitably for that work and has laid the basis for future growth with the e-wallet.

First and foremost, Ken thinks about his business as a business. It is Cellulant itself, and the very act of starting it, that Ken feels delivers the greatest social value. "Listen, Africa is a continent with problems," he said. "I look at people who grew up where I grew up. They are desolate, living in poverty. It's just unbelievable and doesn't have to be the fate of people there. We hope that Cellulant is going to show that businesses can be founded out of no political connections and with no money." Most of all, he's keen to demonstrate that to his employees. As he discussed Cellulant's impact with me, he peered past the thin glass partition of his office to a bullpen of young engineers. "I want them to see you don't need to be the president's cousin to make it. Ken and Bolaji are guys who came around starting with no money and built a successful business. That's going to change the mind-sets of the twenty-something-year-olds out here. That's what I want."

While CEOs are looking at young African talent, emerging African talent is likewise looking at CEOs to see not only what they can pay but the social payoff they can deliver. One North African at Harvard Business School expressed her frustration with older models of African business, in words that resonated with her cohort:

Think about the biggest cement producers, for example. We were giving them subsidized utilities. When asked for environmental measures, they didn't want to conform to it, because their business proposition wasn't built that way. I don't see that as replicable into the future. What I've seen post the revolution, is that there's so much talent in health care, in education, in tech. We want to do away with the conventional industries and how they grew. We don't want to keep selling out our country.

One of her classmates from Nigeria expressed it even more starkly when describing how he would assess business leaders in Africa:

I feel like we can look at a great CEO as someone who is very savvy at finding opportunities and building a company around it. Or we can look at a great CEO as someone who cares about what they are building from a developmental standpoint, not in terms of being a nonprofit but doing things that they believe would actually improve the quality of life of Africans. That's the framework that I use when I assess a CEO.

A business leader who commands that respect is Main One's CEO Funke Opeke. Here is how that same Harvard Business School student from Nigeria expressed it:

I feel anyone like Funke, who had the foresight to see that the next wave of development from Africa relies heavily on information flow, is admirable. To provide high-speed Internet and build the infrastructure that can convert that directly to mobile as opposed to desktops, that is the biggest accomplishment that I've seen in this whole period of African growth. Also, Main One is making concerted efforts at driving down prices to make sure that the bandwidth is within reach. Their goal is to get high-speed Internet to the average African in the next ten years, and I think that's a very incredible thing.

Who doesn't want the talent coming out of business schools to be saying that about her company?

Independently, Funke articulated the same passion for what her firm exists to do. In 2012, Main One embarked on a controversial and sometimes bitter battle to deliver broadband directly to users, bringing the company into direct competition with existing providers. I asked her the rationale for that decision, expecting a purely commercial response. "If we don't ensure our cable is being effectively utilized, then we can't recover the capital that we sank into the ocean. That is definitely true," she said. But then she continued at much greater depth:

We need Internet penetration to more people. I mean Internet penetration to schools, to young people, to small businesses, to be leveraged by government. With so much unemployment, young people in Nigeria are roaming the streets. Give them access to information, perhaps some of them might seek out knowledge that could actually help them acquire skills and become contributors to society. The Internet bridges so many gaps in advanced economies today and unless we start doing that here [in Nigeria], we will continue to remain disadvantaged. That's what we set out to do and we have the bandwidth in the cable system to do it, but the people who need it are not getting it. The objective was to bridge that gap, so I guess we're not successful until we bridge it.

Need is the context in which opportunity is pursued in Africa. For many companies, it is a barrier to entry, limiting them to a luxury niche. For the most successful firms, need is fertile ground in which to attract talent, innovate, and profit.

CHAPTER 5

What Wins

The grass is greener out here, but it's not for the fainthearted.

Bharat Thakrar, CEO, Scangroup

Winning is hard everywhere, and there are as many paths to winning in Africa as there are individuals seeking to succeed. The business leaders I know succeeding in Africa share these traits:

- They embrace uncertainty
- They get their hands dirty
- They build what they need
- They're resilient
- They tailor to local culture

None of these attributes is particular to success only in Africa or frontier markets. They do rise above the throng of characteristics associated with successful people everywhere, such as "hard work." Certainly, hard work is key to success, but no more so in Burundi than the Bronx. The ability to embrace uncertainty matters much more in Burundi than it does in the Bronx.

They Embrace Uncertainty

Business leaders everywhere manage risk. Though executives often talk about them interchangeably, it's useful to distinguish risk from uncertainty. Risk is a known set of possible outcomes, with a known probability for each. Rolling dice has risk. Uncertainty is an unknown set of outcomes, with an unknown probability for each. Doing business in Africa is uncertain.

For many companies, operating in Africa or other frontier markets may actually be a way to mitigate risk. To take just one example, Graham Mackay sees SABMiller's presence in many African countries as a dispersion of risk. "Things happen country by country," he explained. "Taxes go up and down or there is a sudden huge rise in interest rates because the country is overextended. There are policy and economic vicissitudes that you inevitably encounter. The point I would make about Africa and our businesses in Africa is that it helps to have a broad portfolio of many countries."

Uncertainty, by contrast, uncertainty isn't mitigated in advance so much as managed well in real time. The constant need for workarounds, replanning, and accommodation in Africa can be astonishing to the uninitiated. In fact, even experience with uncertainty or tolerance for it isn't really sufficient. Experience means uncertainty won't surprise you—it will just frustrate and exhaust you. To really succeed in the face of that steady drumbeat of uncertainty in Africa or any frontier market, you have to embrace it.

Ken Njoroge embraces uncertainty. His career and the birth of Cellulant were predicated on a massive step into the unknown. In his mid-twenties, Ken was already a partner in 3Mice, an IT professional services company. Ken explained that it was profitable and growing, if not explosively:

We were doing fine, but my billion-dollar-scale ambition was always there. At 3Mice, I began to spend a lot of time on one project, developing new solutions for mobile phones. We didn't have a client on the project. It was internal, and it was losing money, but I could see the scale of growth of African mobile. My partners were comfortable with what we were doing already. They had families and couldn't take a big risk. But for me the greater risk was continuing at that modest level. So, in the end I said, "Listen, I will work just on this one unfinanced project, take it out on my own, and leave you with the money-making part of the business." I gave up my shares in 3Mice and I exited the business.

Jeff Immelt considers a certain level of uncertainty par for the course in fast growth markets. Raised in Ohio by a schoolteacher and a GE division manager, Jeff played football at Finneytown High, "never traveled overseas growing up, and never imagined I would be dealing with Africa." That expectation notwithstanding, Jeff has managed businesses in fast growth markets around the world, and had recently returned from Africa when we first spoke at GE headquarters. Jeff's comfort in frontier markets is palpable, borne of three decades as a GE executive, including twelve years as CEO during which time the company has dramatically expanded its presence in developing Asia, and more recently Africa. He described an occasion when his perspective on uncertainty was brought to the fore:

We were building a joint venture in Angola, and we were stuck in negotiation with our local partner over who owned the land. That issue had delayed consummating our transaction for over a year. Our partner was frustrated, we were frustrated. Now, I'm an old global hand and I've seen how markets form so I have a broader risk tolerance than most. I said to our people, "Listen

Figure 5–1: The Mara Crossing

Source: Eric Inafuku, provided to Wikimedia Commons, August 30 2007.

the opportunities in this country are great, so let's just figure out the risk, and let's go." If you insist on waiting until everything is understood, you will never go. Companies don't do well in Africa because they can never get started. And there's a thousand ways not to get started.

Jeff's experience is consistent with Bharat Thakrar's perspective based on building Scangroup and observing both African and global clients operating on the continent. Bharat explained by way of the following metaphor:*

---

*Animal metaphors tend to proliferate in books on Africa. I have allowed just this one.

I don't know if you know the Mara Crossing? It really describes this very clearly. We have the Mara River that divides the Serengeti. In August, the weather kills the grass on the Tanzanian side. On the Kenyan side it stays green. So the wildebeests migrate in the thousands towards the Kenyan side where the grass is greener, but they have to cross the Mara River and that river is full of crocodiles. They don't know where the crocodiles are. But they cross, to get to the green.

Bharat paused, as if standing on the other side. "The grass is greener out here," he said, "but you have to face the unknown. Africa is not for the fainthearted, and it's not for people who are uncomfortable with the unknown."

Few non-Africans have had as much success in Africa in the last decade as Aidan Heavey of Tullow Oil. Aidan founded Tullow with his own funds, and it has grown into one of the most successful natural resource exploration companies in the world, with $2.3 billion in revenues and a market capitalization in excess of twenty billion dollars. Aidan's the kind of fellow who wouldn't just cross the Mara, he'd be the lead wildebeest leaping into it. This impulse is captured in the way he describes his decision to start Tullow:

My first trip to Africa was to Senegal to look at an oil project. I'd never been to the continent before. When I came down I had no idea what to expect, my images of Africa just being documentaries about wildlife. I was pretty ignorant, I would say. When I went down there to Senegal to start, I just found the place fascinating. From the second I arrived, all the way through, it was amazing. The thought of actually having a business here was like being on holiday all the time, great.

Back in those days, you arrived at the airport and it was a bit intimidating because it wasn't like arriving in London or

New York. The whole atmosphere was so different from what you'd see in Europe. It wasn't like business that I had seen before. It was a bit of excitement there and the people had fresh minds, everything was open. People were offering fresh ideas.

Of course, it was virtually impossible to raise money. Here was a guy who knew nothing about the oil industry from a country that knew nothing about the oil industry, going to a country that had no oil industry to set up an oil company. At the start, it was just a matter of getting the project as far advanced as I could, using my own cash. When I got it to a certain stage, I brought in family and friends. Even they weren't investing in the project; they just invested in me. Then it just worked out quite well.

The ability to embrace uncertainty exists not just in CEOs, of course. A manager who can respond to uncertainty is critical to leading a frontier market operation. I asked Graham Mackay to explain what allows a company like SABMiller to operate profitably in the most uncertain markets, like South Sudan. "Well, that's really tough to put your finger on," he said. After a moment's thought, he concluded that it's this same capacity to handle the unexpected:

There is a sort of self-reliance and a willingness to take things as they come, just to take what the environment deals out to you. You mentioned South Sudan. The chap we've got running South Sudan is an old Africa hand, and he gets called down regularly to pull cobras out of the empty cases coming back. The cobras like coiling up in the empty boxes. The warehousemen are all terrified of snakes and won't go anywhere near them, so he winds up as the snake man.

I hope to import that training technique shortly.

They Get Their Hands Dirty

For many businesspeople from mature markets, frontier markets are exciting. They're also scary. As a result, executives of U.S., European, Japanese, and even Korean companies tend to stay at a safe distance. In their work and especially in their social lives, they often set up pockets or channels of isolation. It's comfortable, but from a commercial standpoint, it's a death knell in Africa.

You need to get your hands dirty to understand the market, precisely because it's so different from your own, and because your assumptions won't work. Bharat Thakrar commented on this behavior. "The other day," he said, "we had a Chinese phone manufacturer in the office and, I asked them, 'Where is your office in Nairobi?' They told me it's in Luthuli Avenue." Luthuli Avenue is where phones and other electronics are sold at retail, in a riot of shops both formal and informal. Bharat went on, "If you ask one of the other larger phone companies where their office is, it's probably in a nice urban area. These guys (the Chinese) are sitting where their market is sitting. That is the strategy you need in Africa." He continued:

> You cannot do this thing of sitting in a board room, developing these plans, bringing expatriates to run the marketing for you or the distribution, who have no understanding of the dynamics. They put their kids in fancy international schools, have some fancy international lifestyle. You've got to go out there and find out what the hell is going on.

When Chris Kirubi invests, he knows what's going on. Chris has been named by *Forbes* as among the twenty most influential business leaders in Africa, and it would be easy to mistake him as a man above the fray. He owns an iconic building in the center of Nairobi, International House, known to all by name alone. When a visitor arrives to see him, the security desk picks up a particular phone and announces, "A guest for the Chairman." Upon entering International House, that is the universal term for Chris Kirubi. The Chairman is coming. The Chairman is in. And once he arrives (in bespoke suit, shirt, and shades)...the Chairman will see you now.

But it would be a mistake to let all that fool you. I asked Chris once if there were any mistakes he made in his life. "Sure," he said, "I was born poor. That's actually quite a mistake: to have to fight to get out of poverty, to support myself, support my relatives, support other people. But when you learn how to get out of it, it's the biggest and the sweetest challenge. If I were born rich, there would be no excitement to remaining rich." Though he could just watch his investments, Chris explained that he prefers his hands dirty:

I always tell my people I'm not a mushroom. A mushroom, you keep in the dark and you feed it dung. I'm not one of those. So in all my businesses, I know as much as my managing directors. Sometimes more, because I talk directly to the ordinary guy. I don't go through liaisons or bureaucrats. I work with the smallest person in our business.

That is the thinking that Chris brought to the microphones of CapitalFM, a popular radio station he bought in 1998 and where he promptly installed himself as a mid-morning disc jockey. He explained why:

That's the lowest level you can be, a DJ. You talk directly to the listener. So if I understand the DJ's issues, what can a managing director know better than me? So I go every day and get on the air. You see, when I first bought the business I found I couldn't contribute to my business. I didn't know the feel of the audience. I didn't know their demand. I didn't know the pressure on those who present programs and every time I told them, "Do something," they told me, "You can't do it that way." The only way to understand, to know it so that you are not an outsider, is to be part of it. Now, nobody can tell me about radio. I know it inside out. I don't like to be a mushroom.

Centum's James Mworia suggested to me that this phenomenon of business leaders getting their hands dirty is not only essential to success, it redefines the role of private equity firms like his. "A great CEO in Africa," he explained, "is deeply engaged in the operations of the business, he has to be to make the company run. That is the CEO we look for. It means that the financial engineering, the investor relations, and even the strategic planning, are tasks that we take on when we invest. That is the division of talent that makes sense in Africa. Today, if we see an African CEO who is very charismatic, and good with investors, but is not deeply engaged in the operations, that is a CEO from whom we would shy away."

They Build What They Need

In the 1990s, Chrysler introduced the concept of the extended enterprise—an enterprise in which the pieces of the operation are interdependent, but owned independently. The interaction of an electricity provider and a manufacturer is a textbook example of the extended enterprise. That is, if the textbook is a U.S. or European one.

In Africa, the extended enterprise needs to be rethought. Vimal Shah explains:

We have all of these companies buying into Africa. There is so much interest. The problem is, most non-African operators don't know how to operate here. Why? Because here an executive operating a company has got to know about the water, the power, the labor, where the people will stay, security, etc. If I was operating in the U.S., all of those would be a given. Where will labor stay? It's a given. Power? It never goes off. Water supply? It's always constant. Security, you don't even have to worry about it. It is the state's concern, it is not my concern. Here you've got to do these things yourself. Your organizational capabilities have to be different in Africa.

Building your own infrastructure can seem an insurmountable obstacle to operating profitably. To be sure, it carries risks and costs that are not typical in more developed markets. Mo Ibrahim describes the challenges, but also the opportunities of building your own infrastructure, and of being first mover in a growth market:

We often had to deal with building telecom backbones to achieve connectivity. We had to build our own microwave networks, satellite base stations, generators, etc. That was tough because it meant that we had to bring forward a higher level of investment, so our initial capital expenditure was high relative to industry standard. But it was offset by the market potential, and we were able to do it sequentially, starting in the capital city and then moving out. Besides, owning the elements of that infrastructure in the long term actually became profitable because instead of leasing it from the government, we eventually leased out the lines and the capacity to other players. In the end, that's proven not a bad investment at all.

There is probably no greater proponent of rethinking the extended enterprise, nor a better example of it, than Vimal Shah and his company, Bidco. That company's story of vertical integration provides insight on why it wins and how it happens.

From Bidco's inception, management had a vision of going "from the soil to the frying pan." They were kept from realizing their vision in early years, as the company was small and access to the inputs for their commodities was difficult. Vimal commented:

If you are in the consumer end of the business alone, you make your money on the branding and the formulations. That might work if the top of the (economic) pyramid is large. Here, the top is very, very small. It's going to grow, but it is going to grow slowly and the middle class has been and is going to grow faster. We looked at it and found selling to that middle we could make a 10 percent premium on our brand. That means the rest of the value has to be gotten from other parts of the chain. So that is where we've gone.

We began with processing soybean, sunflower, and corn, which are locally produced here by small farmers. It is uneconomical to have a plantation for soybean or sunflower. So we built a processing facility for those, and guaranteed the markets and money for five thousand farmers so they would grow more.

With that experience in place, Bidco's leadership wanted to advance further up the value chain into growing, and also expand to a core product—palm oil. Because palm is a plantation crop, it meant a revolution in Bidco's business model. "To achieve commercial returns in palm, you can't do ten acres or even one thousand acres," Vimal explained. "We looked at it globally and found you needed ten thousand hectares (about twenty-five thousand acres). So we began to look around." Vimal eventually found that much space in neighboring Uganda. It was not without a struggle on his part and the government's:

The government of Uganda was advertising in *Newsweek* and *Time*, looking for somebody to invest upstream in palm oil and palm planting—the full agriculture side. When we met with them, they were offering a five thousand-hectare plantation site with thirty-five hundred hectares reserved for outgrowers (small farmers supplementing the plantation's production) to support as a poverty-alleviation program. We said no, it's not economical, and we lost the bid to some guy who didn't know what it would take to succeed. He never got off the ground.

Two years later, they came to us and said, "Are you still interested?" By then, we had partnered with [Malaysian agribusiness] Wilmar, who were already in the plantation business. Wilmar asked, "Ten thousand hectares is viable but what's the growth opportunity?" So we told the government this time that we wanted thirty thousand hectares (seventy-five thousand acres) of commercial plantation.

Though it was six times the acreage the Ugandan government originally planned to approve, the government had spent two years failing with an operator who did not have the vision or experience to succeed at scale. "So," Vimal concludes, "they agreed. We got to work, laying the infrastructure, clearing the land, putting in all the housing, recruiting and training personnel, and building the processing plant. Today we have a fantastic product." As of January 2013, Bidco had twenty thousand acres under cultivation in plantation and another three thousand in outgrower cultivation, and is producing palm oil for the East African market. Bidco now looks at all expansion opportunities through the lens of backward integration. The company has deployed its competencies in Arabica coffee and cut flowers, and is currently examining opportunities for backward integration in cereals.

There is some caution to be expressed with regard to building what you need. Most of Africa is only now developing a robust processing and manufacturing sector, and progress is uneven. As figure 5–2

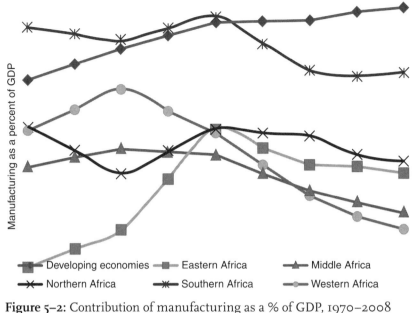

Figure 5–2: Contribution of manufacturing as a % of GDP, 1970–2008

Source: UN Conference on Trade and Development, *Economic Development in Africa Report,*
July 2011.

shows, African industrial production as a portion of GDP hovers
between 5 percent and 15 percent, depending on region and year.
That is far lower than even other emerging market regions.

As a result, governments press for development of processing
plants, distribution networks, and other parts of the value chain.
Sometimes the encouragement is stated as a requirement, and sometimes the expectation is for more than is commercially viable. Aidan
Heavey has negotiated with government on extending his company's operations beyond the elements that are typically core to his
business. In Uganda, the government asked the Tullow-led consor-
tium to build not just an oil production and transport operation, but
also a refining facility. In Aidan's view, the two parties need to find
a middle ground, one that may not be based solely on commercial
concerns:

Every oil company wants to export everything: what makes the most commercial sense is to pipe straight to the Indian Ocean, 1,200 kilometers away, and sell the oil. That's the extreme position you would take as an oil company. However, the government wants a refinery because they're landlocked and strategically they really do need to be independent of another country's refinery. We experienced that firsthand three years ago. The port of Mombasa (Kenya) was closed because of troubles and it prompted a fuel shortage in Uganda. That's why the government is saying they would like a refinery running up to 150,000 barrels per day. We can't get financing for that. We fully understand the strategic requirement, and therefore we think the compromise here is to adjust the development plan to supply a strategic local refinery of 25,000 barrels per day.

Tullow's negotiation with government points to the significant value placed on an extended enterprise, not just by the company, but by other key stakeholders.

They Are Resilient

Nobody succeeds in Africa in a straight line. The minefield of frustration is vast, and I have met hardly anyone successful in Africa who has not endured endless obstacles.

For the most part, these are the everyday obstacles of life with semi-functioning systems. I spoke with a young Nigerian who had returned to the United States from a summer at home, wondering if she had what it takes to succeed in Africa. "It's a hustle," she said, recalling her last job, in Lagos. "Just getting up every day to hustle, not just for business, but for phone, for power, to get from place A to B, is hard." Born and raised in Nigeria, she was no stranger to its pace. But advancing through it, piercing the veil of frustration to build a business, she found daunting. Yet it's precisely that veil that creates a high barrier to entry. Once it's overcome, few follow.

Resilience extends to barriers far greater than the everyday nuisance. Ken Njoroge attributes his success directly to the resilience he learned growing up poor. Really poor, frontier poor. "I think I had engrained in me a mind-set that, despite the odds, you need to get it done. Whether it was not having the money for schoolbooks, or working through school, or working on the Cellulant project for years before it made money, just sticking to it is most of the difference."

Funke Opeke sees resilience in the face of frontier-market obstacles as a key differentiator among her potential business partners. She described the resilience of her Chinese business partners in the face of government obstructions that sometimes frustrate Western executives (including, on occasion, Funke, herself an alumna of Verizon):

For the American businessperson, the degree of frustration must take getting used to. They would think, "We're bringing you money and we're prepared to make this investment, why aren't you clearing the roadblocks for us to help you make it work?" A lot of American companies would just view it as a serious mess and give up. The Chinese come from a newly emerging economy, so they may be more used to dealing with some of those obstacles, and have seen more hardship and so they are more persistent in light of those obstacles.

They Tailor to Local Culture

"I have seen this so many times," Coca-Cola's Neville Isdell said. "A company determines there's an opportunity in Africa and they fly in all their expats, recreate what they have at home, and run it out of their European headquarters. It's expensive because of the pay, the flying around, etc. But mostly it's expensive because it doesn't work."

Neville knows what works. From 2004 to 2008, he was the CEO of the Coca-Cola Company and oversaw a dramatic rebuilding of its worldwide brand. Having spent his career with Coke, Neville retired in 2001. He was asked back by the company in 2004 to help correct its course as CEO, and in 2008 was named by *Beverage Industry* magazine as the sector's CEO of the year.

Neville also knows Africa. Raised in Zambia from the age of ten, he attended the University of Cape Town in South Africa, then returned to Zambia and joined the local Coke bottler at age twenty-three. He came of age in the Coke family, assuming leadership of Coca-Cola's large South Africa operation eight years later before taking on leadership positions worldwide.

Neville says that being local has been central to Coke's success in frontier markets, enabled in part by its model of franchising to local bottlers. "There are always wonderful exceptions but in general expats don't know enough or understand enough about the culture of the society and the way things really work to find a way to do things. This is where the Coca-Cola bottler model proved so valuable and well suited to Africa, because you need good African leadership and African partners to succeed."

While Coca-Cola's business model was well suited to developing a local presence, the traditional model of global oil companies is not. Aidan Heavey feels that starting Tullow from scratch in Senegal proved a massive advantage, in that it kept him from importing approaches and assumptions that would have been wrongheaded:

When we started working with the Senegalese, we didn't have a fixed view on how you do things, because we were a start-up business. We were learning as they were. We set up a Senegalese business, and it was very much a company that was built to work

in that country. That was a winning approach. We hired Senegalese people, we negotiated contracts the way they negotiated contracts. They were thinking a completely different way than we
were. The logic was different and you had to think a slightly different way, but you always got to the solution you needed. I used
to explain to people at the time that it was like back in the '80s,
if you had a big IBM mainframe it wouldn't link with a Mac. If
you had an Irish business you shouldn't assume it would work in
Senegal. That's how you should think about it.

Of course, not every CEO starts with Aidan's *tabula rasa*. Most will
want to integrate their existing cultures and operations with local
expertise. The winning path to that integration is to recruit, train, and
listen to local talent. Mohamed El Kettani describes how Morocco's
Attijariwafa Bank does it:

You don't want to be a Moroccan bank in Congo or Gabon, and
they don't want you to be. When in Congo or Gabon you want
to be Congolese and Gabonese. Human capital is the key. We
are fortunate that, at any one time, there are about ten thousand sub-Saharan students who come to Morocco to study in
our engineering and commercial schools. We recruit from this
population very heavily, finding the best and then putting them
through a two-year program at our headquarters in Casablanca.
We then send them out to the country branch offices. These are
invariably the best flag bearers for the bank in the country.

Bharat Thakrar also points to human capital as the key to effective
integration across regions. In Scangroup's case, the human capital
strategy focused more on lateral movement of employees. In 2011
Scangroup acquired Ogilvy Africa, doubling the firm's size and moving its center of gravity far west of its Nairobi origins. The acquisition

also represented the company's deepest foray to date into franco-phone Africa. Bharat is sanguine about the prospects, but recognizes it will take time and an investment of attention:

> The important thing to do is take your corporate culture and try to translate it to there. Most importantly, you've got to do it slowly. You've got to give it time, because it isn't going to happen overnight. The way you do it is you exchange people and you grow people. The companies that have done that in Nigeria, for example, they don't have the same horror stories everybody else does. It is easier for us to absorb and understand and relate to that culture, because we operated in Ghana two years and we've done well there. We've been in Tanzania, we've been in Uganda. We've come to understand the dynamics of cross-country growth a lot better.

Bharat's reference to corporate culture really can't be overstated. What remains constant across local offices is as important to success in Africa as what must change. I'm familiar with a Fortune 500 company that built up a significant operation in a West African country. In a misguided rush to "Africanize," the company built a cadre of local managers who had no exposure to the company's operations outside their country. The company failed to do precisely what Bharat and Mohamed suggest in different ways: integrate the workforce by osmosis.

The result was disastrous. None of the company's cultural values were present in the West African enterprise. Infighting, corruption, and low expectations were rampant. Staff that sought to reform from within had no support from the parent company. It was an anomaly and dishonor to the parent company, and to the country, where many fine companies with strong values are domestically owned and operated.

I've also worked with a company in the same sector and country that had far greater success with local operations. The company hired and promoted its African managers carefully (and more slowly), invested heavily in training for all staff, and adopted the same safety, environment, and community policies that it has around the world. Perhaps most importantly, the company rotates personnel both into and out of the West African enterprise. In its country headquarters and at its jobsites, the company's culture merges with the local culture. It isn't always harmonious, but it is high functioning and delivers both returns and accolades to the parent company.

Ultimately, there is a core of company values that drives performance across local markets in Africa, as elsewhere. ECP's Tom Gibian has invested in companies from Algeria to Zimbabwe, and describes a conversation he has with nearly every potential investee:

> There usually comes a moment in the discussion when you say to them, "Look, we know this is a unique environment. But we want you to know that, on topics like bribery or the value of our word, you're talking to one company and we all share a single attitude. You may see on our side of the table a Ghanaian, an American, a Nigerian, but we all take the same approach to those topics. To you it might seem very naïve or very simplistic. Maybe it even seems unrealistic; but that's just who we are. If we're to do business together, it has to be who you are too.

That ability to merge core values with local needs has been instrumental in ECP's success engaging private sector investees. As the next chapter explores, it is an important element of the conversation successful firms have with government as well.

CHAPTER 6

What About the Government?

Show that you're here to stay.

Jay Ireland, CEO, GE Africa

Over time, Africa rewards honesty and punishes corruption.

Tom Gibian, CEO, Emerging Capital Partners (2000–2010)

Anyone considering business in Africa asks about the viability of working with governments. It is a first-order consideration for all. For many, it is the deciding factor.

Bob Rubin was straightforward about its impact. "One big challenge," he said as we discussed the challenges a business book on Africa would need to address "is to define a path by which people get comfort that they can operate there without corruption. That's a problem. That they can rely on rule of law is another problem, and that there's some way for them to deal with the risk of political instability is a third."

All of Bob's points are well taken. Political instability persists in parts of Africa, but is on the decline (as described in chapter 2). There is strong evidence that neither African nor emerging market investors perceive that risk to be as daunting as investors from the

United States and Europe do. It's an expensive misperception, and one that I believe will not last.

The lingering questions investors and executives ask most about government in Africa have to do more with the government's direct interaction with businesses, such as:

- Will I have to pay them off?
- If I do not pay them off, what will happen?
- How do I protect my investment from being expropriated?
- How do I protect my investment from unpredictable taxation or regulation?
- Will the courts uphold my contracts?

Addressing these questions requires placing them, and Africa, in context.

These questions are hardly the sole provenance of Africa, or even of frontier markets. Corruption exists everywhere in both illicit forms and those enshrined in law. At the time of this writing, my own country is mired in inaction over spiraling deficits and trapped in a byzantine tax structure in whose corners every powerful lobby hides its favorite tax break. These are the effects of a government corrupted by money.

Many distinguish between these forms of influence in the developed world and "corruption" in Africa. I commend to them the excellent reporting by Ira Glass and his team on how money flows to the U.S. Congress, aired in a March 2012 episode of the broadcast *This American Life*. (http://www.thisamericanlife.org/radio-archives/episode/461/take-the-money-and-run-for-office). Jot down your definition of corruption, whatever it is. Then listen to the first four minutes of this broadcast.

Good governance is worth getting. It's hard to get anywhere, including Africa.

Getting Good Governance for Your Company

In Africa, as in other frontier markets, it's not very useful to plan for (or respond to) corruption in isolation. Corruption usually occurs in conjunction with other governance challenges, like excessive bureaucracy, an absence of working systems, and a shortage of either manpower or skills, or both.

In this regard, businesses can take a page from social science. It's more effective to think about how a business obtains good governance than how it avoids corruption, one manifestation of bad governance. This chapter offers insights on the context for good governance in Africa, and then more specifically on how to build a productive relationship with government within that context.

Government plays a larger role in the life of business in Africa than elsewhere. According to PricewaterhouseCoopers, 21 percent of African CEOs report deriving one-third of revenue or more from government. Fifteen percent of global CEOs do so. Sixty-seven percent of African CEOs see emerging market governments as driving growth for their companies, compared with 52 percent globally.[1]

Not surprisingly, business has been deeply affected when government has performed poorly. James Mworia sees government failure as a toxin that has poisoned the ground in which a generation of great business leaders might have grown. "Steve Jobs is not from Kenya, why?" he asks. "Because the Steve Jobs of this world have not been able to navigate the corruption. If you look at macroeconomic stability, it's a function of the political leadership. There were probably hundreds of such great entrepreneurs and great ideas that could not flourish for this reason." That is the tax and the tragedy of poor governance in Africa.

That tax is coming down, according to the World Bank's *Doing Business* report, the preeminent compilation evaluating the business climate in 183 countries. The 2012 report highlighted the progress of sub-Saharan Africa in particular. In that region, thirty-six of forty-eight countries implemented reforms in 2010–2011 that made it easier to do business, the highest proportion of any region worldwide. The change was not limited to sub-Saharan Africa. Morocco was the most improved country, as it climbed twenty-one places to ninety-four. Four other African countries—São Tomé & Príncipe, Cape Verde, Sierra Leone, and Burundi—were among eleven economies cited as the most improved in ease of doing business across several areas of regulation.

Still, Africa has a long way to go. Mauritius, South Africa, and Tunisia are the only African countries in the top fifty. At the other end of the spectrum, thirteen of the bottom fifteen countries are African. Sub-Saharan Africa continues to be classified as having weak legal institutions and complex and expensive regulatory processes. North Africa fares slightly better on both fronts, but is still behind other developing country regions, and reform momentum there has slowed since the democratic transition set into motion with the Arab Spring.

The result is that Africa, though low in its scores, is rising consistent with other emerging regions and closing the ease-of-doing-business gap with developed economies, as indicated by figure 6-1.

The Relationship of Government and Business

In Africa, as in other frontier markets, it is not by accident that government has not always enabled business. My friend Magatte Diop leads his family office and several companies in Senegal, following a successful global career with Citibank. Magatte enjoys extraordinarily close relations with governments throughout francophone Africa. He explains that, historically, governments have seen themselves in a zero-sum power dynamic with big business. "If you get too big, or too powerful, someone in government would feel threatened

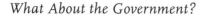

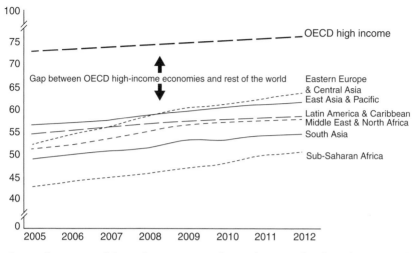

Figure 6–1: Ease of doing business in Africa relative to developed countries*

Source: PricewaterhouseCoopers,*The Africa Business Agenda*, July 2011. By permission.

*The distance to frontier measure shows how near, on average, an economy is to the best performance achieved by any economy on each *Doing Business* indicator since 2005. The measure is normalized to range between 0 and 100, with 100 representing the best performance.

by that," he said, "and that's a fight you could not win. So you had two options: stay out of government's way, or get so big that they can't take you down."

Of course, that's not really two options, it's one. The second strategy of waiting until you are big enough to resist government is often tried, but fatally flawed. You're never sure whether you're big enough until you test it, and you're only as strong as the last test, not the next.* The result is that a few companies have succeeded, while many more lie in ruins. This is not a phenomenon unique to Africa,

---

*A lesson learned well by Russian former business leader Mikhail Khodorkovsky, once the wealthiest man in the country and currently in a prison in Siberia.

but the zero-sum dynamic between government and business certainly has been evident there.

Like Magatte, Sam Jonah's experience with the business–government power dynamic is long and broad, spanning West, South, and East Africa. Sam sees political connections contributing to a shortfall of African capital invested in productive enterprises. "African money, like money everywhere, will flow to where there is the least risk for return," he said. "If a deal is driven primarily by political connections and you can be exposed to less risk as a result, many people will do that rather than fund a project with all the financial and operational risk" of a productive enterprise.

These systemic distortions are complemented by everyday obstacles, no less crippling for being mundane. Sometimes it is simply an absence of systems that breeds government failures. An African student at Harvard Business School had just completed several years working for a Pan-African infrastructure fund. "There is no number to call to get information from the Ministry of Finance," she said. "We would literally fly to Ghana for no other reason than to figure out, 'Where's our contract?' If you don't want to fly every week, you have to know the cell phone numbers of people in the Ministry of Finance in Ghana to gain that clarity." This young executive was quick to add, "We're not greasing people, we're just trying to find information." Her caveat reinforces how easy it is for that broken system to attract corruption.

Even where there is no corruption, failures of governance affect business. In the countries in which Main One's cable has landed, broadband access costs have been cut by 75 percent. Nevertheless, the company routinely finds the expansion of service thwarted by government. CEO Funke Opeke described her company's experience:

You would think in a society where there is so much need and there is so much opportunity, there would be policy in place to guide us towards the right results. Why is it not happening?

To be honest, I sometimes wonder if government officials are trying to help the private sector, or society at large, achieve what they state as their policy goals. They're more there as gate checkers and blockers and fee takers and obstructionists. Society is not holding our government officials to high standards in terms of what their expectations are. That's why Africa is not developed.

The Pernicious Effect of Low Expectations

Funke's comments about obstructionist governmental practices point to one of the most powerful drivers of poor governance: expectations. A friend of mine teaches economics at the University of Nigeria. He once asked his class "What would you think of a man who came from a small town with a modest home, who became minister of finance, and then returned afterwards to that modest house?" "A fool," "incompetent," "mentally retarded," the students replied. "As I feared," the professor said, "we are getting exactly the government we are asking for."

In private conversations, many older Africans have shared a related perspective on expectations. In their communities, a person fortunate enough to have a reliable paycheck is expected to share that good fortune with his or her entire extended family. That can mean forty or more souls depending on one for various forms of financial support. In their view, to be offered the opportunity to earn extra money as a public servant, and then refuse to do so, is an outrage. You are simply reneging on your obligations.

Realistic insight on the drivers of poor governance to date can be sobering, but should not be taken as destiny. Africans do not love corruption, or want bad governance, nor are they destined for it. In fact, the channel is growing wider for good governance, and for businesses to have a relationship with government that is enabling, constructive, and clean.

The Growing Supply of Good Governance

Government in Africa is a changing landscape. Changing in its players, of course, but also changing in its dynamics and prevailing ethos. Running through that landscape is a path of good governance, commitment, and capability. That path, once narrow, is growing wider.

As mentioned above, expectations are a driver of the quality of governance. The replacement of bad governance with good ultimately has as much to do with resetting expectations as with any formal interdiction. The interdiction will never stick, so long as the expectation remains.

Expectations are changing, particularly at the senior level, where governance intersects with popular politics. The democratic reforms discussed in chapter 3 have combined with the Arab Spring to create more pressure on senior leadership to deliver results. "For a long time, governments benefited from low expectations. It was in the interests of many in government to basically say, 'Things really can't be better, so let me get back to taking my share,'" said James I. Mwangi. "People now see that things can be a whole lot better, and they expect their government to help deliver it. My hope is that in the next few years you will see a shift from government being seen as the path to wealth and advancement, to government being responsive to what delivers development and responsive to business needs."

Sam Jonah's top lieutenant, John Barton, has noticed the change in Liberia and Zambia. "When a government leader steps out in opposition to corruption," he said, "as President Sirleaf has in Liberia or President Sata in Zambia, it begins to change that expectation, both from the top down and from the populace towards the government."

What About the Government?

At the same time, senior positions are increasingly held by technocrats with both the skill base and the disposition to deliver good policy. While the trend is not universal, it is vastly more widespread than it was twenty or even ten years ago.

That change is demonstrated in Ken Njoroge's experience winning the farmer subsidy contract in Nigeria discussed in chapter 4. I asked Ken about that contract because it seemed to me a multimillion-dollar tender run by the Nigerian Ministry of Agriculture would be a poster child for poor governance. Ken reports just the opposite. His story is compelling:

I've had a very different experience from what you might expect. I was flying economy to Nigeria, and by the bathroom we bumped into this guy who took an interest in what we were doing with mobile payments. Here was a Nigerian agronomist working with a think tank in Kenya and thinking, "Surely, the payment technology they're developing here can be applied in agriculture."

We started chatting and I said to him, "Forget about what the technology can do, let's define the problem. What's the problem?" We had to pinpoint it. We started sketching the fertilizer sector in his notebook and we talked for over an hour. At the end, he suggested he arrange a meeting with the governor of the Central Bank in Nigeria. I was a little bit skeptical—you know, both of us are in economy class. But we agreed we would e-mail each other. On a Saturday, he called me and he said, "Look, I didn't mention it to you but when we met I was on my way to Nigeria to be confirmed as agriculture minister. That's done. Now I am the minister."

That the minister of agriculture is not a political insider, but rather a technocratic agronomist, speaks to changes occurring in

Africa. The rest of Ken's story points to the widening path for good governance:

> He invited us to Nigeria to present. And just as he had said, there was the Central Bank governor along with several ministers and a state governor. For me, that meeting was so profound. To understand the leadership in a country like Nigeria is not just politicians. They're technocrats. They asked questions about farmer income, looked at the production of food, asked in detail about what the technology is and where it had been proven before. When they were done, they asked, "Can this be ready in time for the next farming season?" and we said yes, we can do it in five months.
>
> At that point, a man from procurement objected that the procurement process alone would preclude that timeline. The group asked whether he would stand in front of the president and explain that the solution was not in place this season because we sat in this room to argue process. We agreed the solution would need to be in place five months hence, in March. That's exactly what happened.

Changes in governance that occur at the top penetrate slowly into the rank and file of civil service. The ministries represented in that meeting with Ken may not always be as focused as the meeting at the top. But the expectation leadership sets is the *sine qua non* for that change to occur.

Once expectations for governance do begin to change, they affect all players, and government's expectations of companies have changed as well. Jay Ireland experiences expectations from African governments that may surprise some. "When I engage with African governments today," Jay said, "a principal concern of the government is whether a company is just in it for the short term, looking for a transactional gain and that's it. They're especially concerned if you don't bring long-lasting employment and growth in the economy."

I pressed Jay a bit on whether that was really the primary concern he heard from government, even in private. "Yeah, that's what they think about," he said. "A lot of people in African government have been abroad, and have seen how it can be. Basically, people are exhausted with not getting what they pay for. That drives more accountable governments, and the preparation of better RFPs.* They're the ones demanding more transparency from us, on the supplier side, in terms of what products we're selling and how we'll deliver training, localize service, and build a long-lasting presence."

Systems Taking Root

As expectations rise for improved governance, the systems that enable that governance also have to grow stronger. Business leaders succeeding in Africa have experienced strengthened systems of governance at the technical, institutional, and strategic level.

Technology contributes to good government not only by increasing its speed but also its accuracy and transparency. "Today we have digital clearance of customs in parts of Africa," noted Jay Ireland. "You swipe your documentation, and it goes into the system. It's not just efficiency. The more you move humans out of a process, the less there are chances for error or corruption." ECP's Tom Gibian described a similar experience on the northern edge of the continent:

If you're using software for your inventory and you're using cranes that can remember where they put something, versus writing it down in a ledger, technology can create efficiencies; capital can create efficiencies. We saw this happening in Egypt,

---

* Requests for proposals

where the government has said new ports will not have union-ized custom officials, which lets them modernize faster. In order to get people to make private investments in port facili-ties, they have had to agree to create a customs infrastructure that will be not dragged into the preexisting muck.

Institutional systems that work well reduce the scope for human inconsistency, including corruption. Functioning institutions also widen the space in which one can operate predictably and cleanly. Centum CEO James Mworia reflected on business in his father's day and his:

We've had a big man mentality in Africa a long time. I remem-ber in the days of Moi,* whenever any big business would come to Kenya, one of the most important visits they would make was to State House to see the president.

I have been CEO since 2008. We've grown from six billion to twenty billion shillings in assets,† and we've made significant investments in regulated industries. I've never had to see a min-ister to work around a system. I don't even know them. I don't need to.

We are building a high-density development on a large par-cel of land on the outskirts of Nairobi. Yet, I never had to see anybody. I put in my application, we submitted our documents, and they were reviewed by the zoning committee as per pro-cedure. We never had to pay a bribe and now we are carrying on with the project. There has been so much change in this regard, but there's probably a perception issue internationally

---

* Daniel Arap Moi, president of Kenya from 1978 to 2002
† 20 billion Kenyan shillings is $230 million

and even among some people locally. Some people don't realize how much this has changed.

In Mo Ibrahim's experience, change has extended even into the courts, institutions that many would assume are a bastion of poor governance on every dimension. He describes his experience in three African court systems, litigating against the government itself. While few businesses wish to be in litigation with the government, it's worth noting that Mo felt he could bring suit and win:

We have taken at least three governments to court in Africa and we won every case. In Zambia, for instance, we were asked to hand back some bandwidth, because of an alteration to our license. We refused because we had a clean agreement with the government, won in open tender. Our country CEO called me and said, "We're going to court." As it happens I was invited to a lunch with the president of Zambia that day. I went off to the luncheon and told the president, "Well, sir, guess what? We'll be testing the courts in your country." I explained the situation to him and he said, "You're absolutely right to take us to court." He let it proceed as normal. We had that experience in Zambia, in Malawi, and in Chad, and won in all three courts. People should not think that Africa is the Wild West. What happens when you take the government in China to court?

Not every business leader is prepared to rely on courts in Africa. Many build into their contracts an alternative dispute-resolution mechanism such as binding arbitration in a neutral venue. Nonetheless, Celtel's experience, even in a remote market like Chad, speaks to the widening path of good governance.

Good government can be seen even at the most strategic level, in ways that have a material impact on businesses. Chapter 2 describes the effect that the Kenyan government's Vision 2030 has on James Mworia's ability to raise capital for the Two Rivers development. James is not the only one who speaks of that strategy. Unsolicited, Kenyan CEOs raise it, reference it, and plan around it. Leaders in other countries emulate it.

I asked Centum's James Mworia why. "Typically, visions like that are used to politically hoodwink people," he said. "With this plan, they get done." He continued:

If I look at the economic pillar of Vision 2030, there were key infrastructure projects identified. The expansion of the Thika highway—that has been done. Upgrading the airport—that is being done. Upgrading the Port of Mombasa—that is being done. The Lamu pipeline—that is underway. There was a political pillar, and part of that political pillar was enactment of a new constitution. That has happened. There were constitutional offices like the attorney general for which fresh appointments were going to be made. Those have happened. There was going to be a vetting of the judges. That has happened, very publicly.

Because so much is being created anew in Africa, there is ample opportunity to execute plans very visibly, or to fail to do so with equal visibility. When empowered constituents begin to depend on government's plan, it reduces the opportunity for poor or arbitrary decision making or no decision making at all. While no plan eliminates poor governance, a good plan grows the space in which sound decision making takes place.

The Nongovernment Economy Is Growing

Centum's Two Rivers development displays another change under-way throughout Africa: the growth of formal economic activity outside of government. According to the African Development Bank's *2012 African Development Report*, from 1996 to 2008, the private sector represented more than 80 percent of total production, two-thirds of total investment, and three-fourths of total credit in Africa. Government is still important to business, but its dominance of production and consumption is going down.

The diffusion of economic activity away from the state has a profound effect on the relationship of businesses with government. James Mworia explains its effect on his business:

If you look prior to 2000, the government was the largest customer. In the absence of a middle class, you only became rich by doing business with government. You had multinationals who were doing okay, and they mostly enjoyed quite sizable monopolies. The breweries, the sugar companies, the consumer goods; those were also quasi-monopolies and to enjoy those, you went through government. Access to capital was very difficult for a lot of people. Outside of the very informal sectors of trade, for you to do any significant business, you needed to interact with government for that as well.

The game changes when you look at the numbers I showed you. In the narrow radius of our retail catchment area, there's a market spending three billion shillings* a month. That customer base has nothing to do with government. That mind shift may not have taken place in an older generation of Kenyans, to realize that government is less and less relevant in enterprise, that it's probably a better opportunity serving the ordinary person. That's the beauty of an economic democracy.

This evolution of government's relationship with business carries

---

*Three billion Kenyan shillings is about $35 million.

risk of a backlash. As Magatte Diop mentioned, governments in Africa have often seen themselves in a power dynamic with business where one's gain is the other's loss.

Private equity leader Tom Gibian recognizes that historical phenomenon. In his view, it's being slowly displaced, driven by a profound demonstration effect from other emerging markets. Tom participated in those markets before coming to Africa, and describes trends there that are now emulated in Africa:

A deep, influential driver of growth is simply the example that other emerging markets established, and that has inspired improved governance in Africa. It started with cell phones and has gone on to other allocations of spectrum and licenses as the right for private businesses to participate has expanded. It's been really important that the government has viewed their role following these privatizations as primarily collecting a royalty, and not a party to the business. Because they watched what happened in India and China and Latin America, they understood there was a powerful incentive for the government not to demand total control and not to intermediate the transaction between the customer and the service provider. Because mobile telephony was initially seen as a toy, a fad, or a rich man's indulgence, the rationale to intermediate every transaction was removed. Recall that in 2000, the experts were projecting 5 percent or so penetration for most African countries. The stunning success of mobile phones has had a very positive demonstration effect of allowing the private sector to be the engine of growth in at least certain areas.

Perhaps most importantly, it actually stabilized the political structure rather than disrupting it. It is the grinding poverty, pervasive corruption, and the lack of opportunity or hope associated with a ruling group's insistence on total control that creates true weakness. This idea that the loss of control of any important element of the economy weakens the hold of the ruling party, I think is turned on its head by the examples in Asia, and in Latin America.

Changing expectations, improved systems, and a fundamental realignment of the state's role in the economy are all shifts that take place slowly and unevenly, and countercurrents to these trends persist throughout the continent. Taken as a whole, however, they widen the path in which good (and clean) governance arises. Today, that path is wide enough in Africa for any company to walk in it.

Getting Good Governance for Your Company

Every business leader participating in *Success in Africa* has found it possible to succeed in Africa and have a productive, transparent relationship with government. That does not mean that every company succeeding in Africa has chosen that path. I know many business leaders with an opaque (and in my view, corrupt) relationship with government. Some of them are succeeding wildly. I also know business leaders who have a hostile and unproductive relationship with government. Few of them are succeeding. Ironically, there's also a fair bit of overlap of business leaders who both engage in corruption *and* have a dreadful relationship with government.*

Most globally competitive business leaders I know have determined that it's worthwhile to have a productive and transparent relationship with government. Those relationships share a few common characteristics. The successful relationships I've seen are all long term, collaborative, broad based, and consistent. None of these

---

*That there may be a causal link between the two is an interesting theme.

characteristics is surprising, but I find there's insight to be gained from how successful CEOs implement them.

Long-Term Engagement

Governments in Africa are like governments elsewhere in their need to meet short-term political needs. What distinguishes frontier market governments is how often they value long-term commitment by companies.

An example from outside Africa helps shed light on the point. A friend of mine worked with one of the world's top three investment banks in the early 1990s. The bank was expanding in Mexico when that country went through a financial crisis in 1994 driven by a rapid and deep devaluation of the Mexican peso. The bank moved aggressively to reduce its exposure to all Mexican entities, including government. The federal government of Mexico quietly sent a message to the bank saying, "We have the liquidity to pay you now. But if we do, you will never do business with us again." The bank took its money. The government, backed by the U.S. Treasury, proved liquid and the peso recovered quickly. Despite the investment bank's unrivaled expertise, network, and reputation, it has never recovered its position in the Mexican market to this day, nineteen years and $738 billion in Mexican growth later.[2]

By contrast, GE's Jay Ireland is betting on African governments rewarding long-term commitment. "As a market, Africa has gained attention," Jay explained. "Governments are used to seeing companies come by. So what are we bringing that's different? If you can be seen as a company engaged in the country's long-term development, and explain the benefits you and your team bring to support that development, it shows real commitment. Most importantly, it shows that you're here to stay."

To that end, GE has developed "company-country" dialogues in two of its core African markets, Nigeria and Kenya. The dialogues are based on the long-term development needs of the country and assume a long-term presence by GE, independent of any single transaction. GE reinforces its message of long-term commitment by focusing the dialogue not only on product, but on the creation of skills, employment, and enterprises in the national economy at scale, and well beyond its own workforce. The results of that dialogue include, but are not limited to, GE equipment sales and revenue generation. In the case of Nigeria, GE is also investing in a manufacturing facility, supplier development, and extensive technical training operations. GE's approach provides a model for several aspects of a productive relationship with frontier market governments.

Olam is similarly pursuing long-term strategies in core African markets that include new investments in plantations, processing plants, and brands. In early 2013, investor pressure grew on Olam to gear down debt and create more cash flow. Even as it did, Olam stepped up local and national engagement in Africa to assure it communicated its sustained commitment to the investments it was making.

Collaboration, Not Reciprocity

A successful relationship with government means more than delivering value to government for value returned. That is reciprocal, but not collaborative, and it devolves quickly into a transactional tit-for-tat. That's a road to inevitable disappointment.

The path to a productive relationship with frontier market governments is based on pursuing goals together, with accountability for both parties. GE's Jeff Immelt has found this collaboration overcomes many of the shortcomings that otherwise inhibit companies from entering fast growth markets. He described his perspective on the centrality of a collaborative relationship with government:

> If we've looked at a country and see there's opportunity, and that the reward outweighs the risk, then we want to invest. And really, if we see that the government is there with us, and that people who can drive change have skin in the game, then we'd say, OK, we're good to go. Let's go." But you need a pitcher and a catcher. You can't be a pitcher with no catcher.

Jay Ireland elaborated on how a collaborative relationship plays out in GE's company-country dialogue process:

> Part of the challenge is that there needs to be accountability on both sides. At the highest level, government controls the environment that allows business to grow, so if our supply chain is going to create jobs, it needs that good environment. Then, at the project level, the government needs to put in land and permits, etc. Part of the discussion is about who is your government counterpart, and that takes a lot of time. You have to know that the people who go into the meeting have the authority to get things done, and then there has to be measurable progress on both sides.

I work with one Fortune 200 company that maintains a successful relationship with its host African government despite steep competition for a limited-term license. Every time the company and the government agree on a project, they build a set of obligations on each party and the data to measure progress. The relationship is governed by a standing joint body with clear lines of authority. That is not how the relationship began, and it took at least a year before both parties internalized the idea that how they fulfilled their obligations would advance or halt the project. Today, that is clearly understood.

A collaborative framework can take the place of a reciprocal one. Throughout Africa, SABMiller is seeking to increase the use of local ingredients in its brands to generate employment. If the relationship were reciprocal, or a tit-for-tat, the project would likely fail. Graham Mackay described the collaborative relationship needed with government:

> Beer is different from other alcohol types. It has a very high local employment multiplier because of its bulk agricultural inputs and diffuse distribution network. But by far the largest part of the beer's price is tax. So, in order to create that employment multiplier effect inside the country we ask government to tax the local product at a lower rate, because if they do that, the economics of farming locally can work.

Collaboration also allows the business to socialize government to market dynamics that affect the project. Because of the strong left-leaning past of many African countries, many government officials have had limited exposure to markets. On occasion, Graham Mackay has found that to be the case, and the collaboration has helped. "Governments are disinclined to believe in price elasticity," he said. "They'll come with the point of view that we're just the passive collector of taxes, so what skin is it off our nose if the tax is higher or lower? But as a price factor, it makes the difference between success and failure in a business. That takes time to demonstrate and discuss."

Broad Participation

In Africa as elsewhere, every marginal partner added to a process increases its complexity. Nonetheless, productive transparent relationships with government in Africa (as in other frontier markets) often depend on expanding the relationship within government, within the business, and to other organizations.

When developing its company-country agreements, GE engages at several levels of government. Because GE is active in many sectors, its initial primary contacts are often in the office of the head of state or planning ministry. Yet even at this stage, both individual ministries and individual GE business units are involved. Jay recalls that "One of our early lessons was that if you don't have those actors engaged from the outset, you are asking for it to go nowhere."

Once a broad framework is in place, the primary point of contact shifts to the ministerial level, and is often conducted by individual business units within GE. "Still," Jay explained, "we always keep a connection at senior levels, to ensure there is political authority, and someone who is asking for results."

Multiple layers of engagement also insulate against failures of will or transparency. "As you go down into the depth of the ministries, you can find new challenges," said Jay. "You may find permits slowed, items held up in customs. If you can get that top-level authority, it helps smooth those out."

Both Nigeria's Tony Elumelu and Kenya's Vimal Shah dedicate significant CEO time to business–government commissions, both as a vehicle to support government goals and as a means of pursuing better enabling environments for their business.

Such commissions are common in developed economies, but they have a different and more central role in Africa. As Graham Mackay pointed out, many senior African officials have had limited exposure to market dynamics. Yet today most are interested in attracting trade and investment. That creates a favorable dynamic for such commissions if they're constructed well and focused on specific challenges. Vimal Shah is quite practical about why he invests in commissions:

Listen, you don't live in a tiger's cage and start fighting it. You say fine, let's make peace. I find the way to work it with governments here is to work through associations, work through lobbying bodies. You form a good association of like-minded people and then you come together and you become a force in that sense, and then you've got similarities being shared, experiences being shared. Government will want that advice and will listen.

Vimal has found that these engagements also help overcome the zero-sum phenomenon that can divide big business and government:

Evidence-based lobbying is being encouraged a lot more now. You get evidence, you do benchmarking, and you can engage in co-operative leadership with people in government. There are many bodies that the government has now created where the private sector and government sit together and engage. I sit on some of those, like the National Economic & Social Council. You are communicating ideas of how to govern, how to change things around. And they do drive a lot of change. People who have spent their lives in formal government employment, the government minister or the permanent secretary, can have a one-track mind of how to get things done. When you have these commissions they get different views. On the National Economic and Social Council, we have fifteen or sixteen private-sector people representing different pillars of the economy, including services and manufacturing; and you have got all of these PSs and ministers sitting across the table from you as colleagues. Without fear or favor, you are able to question and discuss openly issues and new ideas of where to go in this country. That has given it a lot of credibility.

As Vimal's comment suggests, government–business commissions provide an opportunity for most businesses that they did not have earlier in the post-colonial era. Favored elites always had unfettered access to governments, but the majority of business leaders in many countries were not only shut out, they were at some risk if they took exception to government policy, even on technical grounds. Tony Elumelu finds his recent participation in Nigeria's commissions moves past that history:

> For a long time, we in the private sector allowed our government to set policies that affect us. Sometimes we stayed silent, sometimes we complained privately, but we did not engage. The government policies can be stifling, but we did not engage the government on how to do it better.
>
> For instance, in conjunction with the Nigerian government, we have put in place a national competitiveness council of which I am the vice chairman, through which we are articulating business-enabling policies that will make Nigeria score better in the World Bank Ease of Doing Business rankings. That is the kind of engagement I like to have with government, to shape broad policy. More African public sector leaders are asking to engage and are more receptive than they have been in the past. That's all to the good. We are answering that call.

Consistent Posture

"I think when you go into any country you need to start off the way you intend to continue." That view, expressed by Tullow's Aidan Heavey, captures the perspective of nearly every business leader participating in this book. Aidan's view, is unequivocal:

We took a view right from day one that everything that we did would be transparent. We didn't get involved in any corruption. That's a key point in Africa. You start off doing things properly and people respect you for it. With that approach, I'll tell you, you can work in any country and work cleanly. There are corrupt businesses and corrupt people, but you don't have to deal with them. There's enough people there who want to do things properly, who are fed up with corruption in their countries. If you want proof of it, look at Tullow. Today we're a $21 billion company working in Africa. You can do it.

In my view, it's not the only path to commercial success, but I believe it is a viable one, and one that is becoming progressively more viable in more places. Moreover, consistency is not a matter of ethics alone. Many executives consider it sound business judgment. "When you're there for the long haul," Aidan said, "politicians change, people change. I think if you look at the companies that get involved in all of this, they're the ones that come a cropper."

Tom Gibian's business is vastly different from Aidan's, but his perspective is precisely the same:

Over a period of time, you just find that attracting investors, attracting good clients, and preserving your reputation all have financial value that you want to protect. Never mind being able to sleep well at night; never mind trying to be a role model for your kids. You look at numbers, you run it through your analysis, and you just simply conclude that Africa over time rewards honesty and punishes corruption. Maybe not in every single transaction, but over time.

It's a perspective shared by African business leaders as well. Mo Ibrahim wrote recently of his approach when founding and operating

Celtel. The practices Celtel put in place reinforce the importance of consistency to success:

> From the beginning we needed a plan to deal with the percep-
> tion of Africa as corrupt. We insisted on accepting only licenses
> we had won in an open bidding process; we would never accept
> them if they were offered under the table or after dining out
> with some prime minister. (We declined to pursue opportuni-
> ties in Guinea and Angola for related reasons.) To make sure
> that no one in the company tried to take matters into his own
> hands, we instituted a rule that the full board had to sign off on
> any expense over $30,000. It wasn't easy to hold this line, but in
> the end it was very helpful, because it enabled us to build a com-
> pany that was completely transparent. Board members helped
> prevent corruption, too. For example, Salim,* the secretary
> general of the Organization of African Unity [now the African
> Union] for twelve years, is so well respected across the continent
> that if an official hinted at a bribe, he could call the right govern-
> ment person and frame the situation as an embarrassment to
> Africa. That was usually enough to stop it. Our directors' con-
> nections created a protective layer around our company.[3]

I spoke with Mo more about the topic a few weeks after his views were published. I pressed him on whether a consistent pattern of transparency really led to superior profits. "Listen," he said, leaning in, "I always found at the end of the day, it was simply good business. Corruption is a tax, and an unpredictable one at that."

Mo extends his message on corruption into his philanthropic work. The Ibrahim Foundation tracks and celebrates good governance, and also calls out governance shortcomings.

---

* Salim Ahmed Salim, the former prime minister of Tanzania

That can make Mo's job a tough one. On the one hand, he has a unique role in speaking to the global business community and fostering interest in Africa as an attractive place to do business. On the other, his is the single most effective voice in the fight against corruption in Africa.

The dichotomy came to a head in 2012 when the Ibrahim Foundation, for the third time in six years, declined to offer its prize for clean leadership in Africa to anyone. Mo and the foundation received a large ration of criticism for sending the wrong message about Africa. It was even suggested the prize be abolished.

"We need to keep the bar high," Mo told me later. "I refuse to accept that Africa needs a lower standard in anything, including transparency. When we awarded the prize to Pires, to Mogae, and to Chissano,* it meant a lot. I won't diminish their accomplishments or the prize by setting a new standard each year."

In my view, that is precisely the correct and accurate message to send about Africa today.

---

*The recipients to date of the Ibrahim Prize; they are, respectively, Presidents Joaquim Alberto Chissano of Mozambique, Festus Gontebanye Mogae of Botswana, and Pedro de Verona Rodrigues Pires of Cape Verde

CHAPTER 7

What About China?

I'll love you, dear, I'll love you/till China and Africa meet.

W.H. Auden

The most important thing for Africa about China is it's not Europe.

Tom Gibian, CEO, Emerging Capital Partners (2000–10)

The Story We Don't See

In 2008, I sat in a Washington, D.C., ballroom with an august group of U.S. and African business leaders to celebrate U.S.–Africa business ties. As is often the case with august groupings in D.C. ballrooms, the most anticipated speaker was a former statesman of the highest order. For reasons that will be clear shortly, I'll not name him.

The speaker rose and the august grew silent. He spoke passionately and intelligently about world affairs, growth, opportunity, and Africa. Then he said this: "I know that China has grown to be a significant source of trade and investment for you in Africa. Let me tell you, China is not your friend. They are in Africa for one reason, to make money. It's not like us."

That statement struck me as a failure of self-reflection, strategic savvy, and simple fact. The only point I could agree with is that China is in Africa for the money, which most Africans I know understand and respect. I took a quick visual survey around the room, pausing at some of the faces I knew. A few displayed surprise. Most were either too polite to show it or had simply heard it often enough to be used to it.

China's role in Africa is vastly covered in media. A Google search on "China and Africa" yields 2 billion hits (about nine times more than "African success" or any similar variant). Similarly, there are 2.2 million scholarly articles on Africa and China.[1] I often feel we read more about Chinese success in Africa than we do about African success in Africa. There are many examples, but I'll cite one that surprised me in particular, in part because I have so much respect for the author. In June 2012, Nicholas Kristof wrote a column in the *New York Times* on the rise of Africa.[2] Mr. Kristof is justly a two-time Pulitzer Prize winner who speaks truth to power often, and has a long-term commitment to covering Africa. "Africa on the Rise" was a terrific column and pivotal in how the media covers Africa. The only point on which I would take issue with the column is that the only company mentioned is the Nien Hsing Textile Co., based in Taiwan with a factory in Lesotho. I would love to travel someday with Mr. Kristof to meet with African business leaders like those in this book.

Mr. Kristof's column was good in many other ways, not least in describing the benefits to Africa of the Nien Hsing investment. If you read most Western press reports and government statements about China's presence in Africa, you will emerge with the impression that China's commercial success in Africa does not benefit Africans, squeezes others out of Africa, and is built on China's willingness to bribe. The men and women succeeding in Africa tell a different part of that story, one of Chinese companies winning mostly for good reasons, in ways that mostly benefit Africa and even other trading partners.

Much of the debate of whether China is good for Africa seems to take place in neither China nor Africa. Mostly, it takes place in the

West. I used to have a very street-savvy friend named Alfonso who knew how to make things plain. Alfonso was deeply engaged with me in a late-night debate when his partner, Jack, intervened to correct him on some point. "No sir!" Alfonso said, with a wave of his finger, "This is an A–B conversation. C yourself out of it."

I can imagine either the Chinese or the Africans suggesting we C ourselves out of it. Mo Ibrahim makes a very simple but powerful point in this regard. "U.S. friends talk to us as if Africa has been an unfaithful business partner that now is trading with China, and that we are at risk from it," Mo said. "But the number one trading partner of China is the United States. So, why is it so good for the United States to trade with China and it's bad for Africa?"

I found that a hard question to answer, especially given the questioner, among the most outspoken voices for good deals for the African public. Kenya's Chris Kirubi is likewise outspoken, daily on his radio show and several times a day via Twitter. Chris captured well the spirit I find among most African business leaders on this matter, asking, "The shoe you are not wearing, why should it pinch you?"

Critics point to China's extensive infrastructure-for-oil loans as a unique source of ill-gotten gains for both China and corrupt African leaders. Though I am not an expert on public sector financing, it is far from clear to me that the evidence supports that assertion as broadly as it is made.*

---

*Someone who is expert on that topic is Johns Hopkins professor Deborah Brautigam. She is one of the few scholars equally at home in China, Africa, and a public finance term sheet. See her scholarly writings at http://www.sais-jhu .edu/faculty-and-scholarship/faculty-profiles/deborah-br%C3%A4utigam-phd or her blog www.chinaafricarealstory.com. See also the work of retired U.S. diplomat David Shinn, best accessed via his personal blog, http://davidshinn .blogspot.com. Each presents a dimension of the China–Africa public sector relationship.

Why the Chinese Win

Commerce is much clearer to me. And in commercial matters, the Chinese win because they deserve to. The Chinese win in Africa because they manage uncertainty well, get their hands dirty, demonstrate remarkable resilience, and localize their business model: The characteristics common to most successful CEOs in Africa, regardless of their origin.

Vimal Shah has seen firsthand Chinese willingness to embrace uncertainty. He describes his experience raising funds in Beijing and New York:

> Let me tell you, the biggest problem in Africa is capital formation. You have an abundance of entrepreneurs, people who can think right, and with ideas that can work, but they don't have access to funds. I went to Wall Street for funding once, and they said, "Look, if you want a billion dollars you can collect that for a viable project in the U.S. in a week's time. The minute you say Africa and you say a billion dollars—it will take you years." China is coming to us and saying, "Okay, fine, here we are. We have capital. Let's do things." Africa needs this.

African business leaders often see the Chinese bringing an immediacy to the projects that underpin future growth. "In Africa, we have suffered because the West only will fund based on past demand," says James Mwangi. "We need to be able to build based on what will be, on future demand. This they have a hard time doing."

Anticipated demand is what drives many of Africa's most important development projects. Infrastructure projects, in particular, are critical to Africa's growth and must be driven based on anticipated (and uncertain) demand. Few Western companies have demonstrated they are prepared to take on that level of uncertainty.

The Chinese are prepared to take on that level of uncertainty. From 2001 to 2010, the World Bank estimates that official Chinese entities committed an estimated $35 billion to financing infrastructure projects.[*,3] In most cases, these loans are secured by anticipated future revenues. Vimal Shah reflects on Chinese companies' appetite for the $24 billion Lamu Port and Southern Sudan–Ethiopia Transport Corridor (LAPSSET), a project integrating port, rail, road, and pipeline:

Look at LAPSSET, one of our more important projects for the whole of East Africa. It goes across the roads, railways, and pipelines. Here, in Africa, we need these projects. The Chinese tell us they can design, build, own, and finance it—the whole lot. Pretty quickly, they are able to look at the project and see we can afford this with the petroleum that will be coming out of South Sudan. They are willing to have that concession and charge a toll so they can get their revenue stream. They are ready to advance to concession agreements on this basis.

Then we (the Kenyan government) have also come to the IMF and the World Bank for funding. Their response was, "Well, we will look at it. First we need to see whether this is really feasible or not." What I see is an "analysis paralysis."

Both Funke Opeke and Phuthuma Nhleko have had major supply contracts with Chinese companies as they moved into new markets, and speak well of the experience. "What I would say is

---

* Based on the data of the World Bank's Public–Private Infrastructure Advisory Facility, which takes the approach of only reporting projects that are reported by the Chinese press, whose values could be confirmed by Chinese sources and have been confirmed as signed

the Chinese want it more," Funke said. "Yes, they have the support of the state behind them, but they are very eager to get African business."

Phuthuma also found Chinese companies a welcome addition to the African landscape. They entered foreign markets at highly competitive prices, and showed a willingness to be hands on in even the toughest places, where Western providers were more circumspect in deploying personnel because of security issues. As an example, he reflected on MTN's successful relationship with certain Chinese telecommunications equipment providers.

I would like to believe that MTN was one of the first major customers for some of the Chinese telecoms companies. We were one of their customers that created momentum in their introduction to telecoms in Africa, particularly in Nigeria. I felt that was fantastic for us and for Africa because, quite frankly, they brought down the pricing of telecom equipment, particularly the switches and base stations. They put huge pricing pressure on equipment and software, which had been the exclusive domain of European and American suppliers. From an operator's perspective, the entrance of the Chinese was most welcome. It brought some robust competition into the market.

It wasn't just price. We found the Chinese to have far more capacity to deploy in difficult terrain than, for example, their European competitors. MTN's footprint covers some very difficult regions in remote parts of Afghanistan, for instance. The terrain was difficult, the elements unfriendly, security a challenge, and consequently it is not always easy to get technicians out there who can help. We found the Chinese companies were in a better position to be able to deal with those sets of conditions.

China has demonstrated true resilience in the African market, as a country, in its companies, and even on the individual level. As a nation, China has been actively engaged in Africa's development as a matter of policy continuously since the 1960s. GE's Jay Ireland recalls that "just as I was getting my new job, we visited the Tanzanian rail officials to discuss engineering support for them. When I got back to the States, I met a Chinese engineer and mentioned I was moving to Africa. He said, "Oh, I used to live there, twenty years ago. We had an engineering support program for the railroad in Tanzania." I walked away and said to myself, "Okay, that's what people don't know. They've been here doing this for a while."

Trade statistics illustrate the dramatic deepening of this relationship. In 1960, China's trade with Africa was $100 million. By 1990, trade between Africa and China had increased tenfold to U.S. $1 billion. That is when the rapid change really began. Chinese-African trade increased tenfold again during the 1990s and then did it *again* in the 2000s. It reached $55 billion in 2006, making it second only to the United States, and in 2009, Chinese trade reached $91 billion, which surpassed the U.S.[4] Trade was $166 billion in 2011, and Standard Bank forecast trade to surpass $200 billion in 2012.[5] Figure 7–1 shows the last decade.

That kind of long-term commitment extends to Chinese companies (many of which are state-owned or state-influenced). One manifestation is in the duration of loans available from Chinese lenders, which can be two to three times as long as those available from Western lenders.[6] Phuthuma, echoing many other African business leaders, sees a comparatively longer-term commitment in the individual Chinese companies with whom he has worked. "Chinese companies will tend to take a very long-term view, a more strategic view compared to their Western competitors," he said.

I asked Phuthuma to what he ascribed that long-term view. Aside from culture, which he thought quite important, he associated it

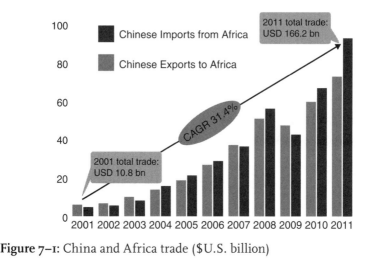

Figure 7–1: China and Africa trade ($U.S. billion)

Source: CEIC, "Regional Focus: CHINA–AFRICA," *The China Analyst*, April 2012.

with the Chinese model of state capitalism, a model most Westerners would assume inhibits good business practice. Not necessarily
so. Phuthuma explained that, "I would think a company that has to
do quarterly reporting on the stock exchange looks at life very differently from a company that doesn't have to do that. So clearly, if companies have a very different model, like the Chinese model, it will
influence the way that they approach markets."

While the Chinese model has advantages that benefit Africa, neither Phuthuma nor the other CEOs commenting on China expressed
a preference for the Chinese model of state capitalism, which has
drawbacks as well. Jeff Immelt, whose company competes directly
with Chinese infrastructure providers, addressed these:

Clearly China has beaten us to the punch in Africa, but they
are playing with the house's money. If someone comes in and
brings $30 million to build a port with thousands of Chinese
laborers, what's learned in that country? Is that long term?
Whereas if we come in and say we're going to do a venture on

150

commercial terms and we're going to train people here, I would say that's long term. To win, we have to train people, we have to produce locally, we have to have joint ventures with local partners. I think our value proposition is powerful, and it's different than China's.

Jeff's point is well taken. Nonetheless, the greatest source of Chinese competitiveness may be the least tangible. One hears it repeatedly from African business leaders: the Chinese treat Africans as equals.

Sam Jonah competes with the Chinese for mineral resources, but respects the way they do business in Africa. "They come offering a transaction," he said. "They are seeking political relations and access to minerals, and in exchange they build infrastructure. That is not a bad thing. What the Americans do not see is that we are more comfortable with an exchange of that kind, a transaction among equals, than we are with aid."

That perspective—that the Chinese afford Africans the dignity of equality—is echoed by many African business leaders. It's evident in civil society as well. Fred Swaniker is the visionary founder of the African Leadership Network, a continent-wide association of rising African leaders under the age of forty-five. When we spoke, Fred had just led fifteen of these future African leaders to the PRC. Like Funke Opeke, he finds the Chinese can see Africa's future because they so vividly recall their own past:

The Chinese, unlike Western companies, see Africa as an investment, not charity. And I can understand why. Average Westerners going to Africa today, in their lifetime, can never remember a time where their country looked like Africa, and so can't imagine that something like Africa could actually be a business opportunity. They just think, "Oh, all these poor people. I need to help them. This is not a place I should be thinking about investing. I shouldn't be coming to make money here. I really just need to help these people."

The average Chinese person walking into Africa remembers a time when China looked like Africa, thirty years ago. Their reaction is, "Wow, this is another chance for us to do it again. We can invest here. We can make money." They see it as a business opportunity. That's why I think that Africa can engage with China in a very different way.

The American statesman who cautioned African businessmen that the Chinese wanted only one thing was right. What he failed to perceive was that many Africans want it right back.

Looking Ahead

Chinese companies are winning opportunities in Africa. In some sectors, they're taking business from Western competitors. While difficult for those companies, the net effect will be markets that work well and competitors that work harder.

Having said that, much of China's commercial engagement in Africa is creating opportunities for other companies. Tullow's Aidan Heavey is among the CEOs who have found Chinese companies to be valuable partners in their multibillion-dollar African projects. In 2012, Tullow Oil entered into a $2.9 billion partnership with the French company Total and the Chinese petroleum giant CNOOC (China National Offshore Oil Corporation) to develop Uganda's oil fields. From Aidan's perspective, the Chinese are proving good partners for him and for Uganda, reflecting many of the characteristics described above: "We found the negotiations with CNOOC very, very good. Since they farmed in,* they've been a great partner. When they

---

* A trade term for joining in the development of an oil or gas producing asset

get involved in a project, they get the project done, and what they are looking at in Africa is very much long term. In our case, the Chinese are going to build an express highway from Entebbe to Kampala. That's going to be a godsend."

Several business leaders succeeding in Africa see the Chinese efforts as somewhat complementary to Western business interests. In particular, the Chinese are seen as executing infrastructure projects that are beyond the scope of others, and which enable all other firms to operate. Aidan Heavey's words capture the sentiment of many:

I also wouldn't see the Chinese as something that other countries should be afraid of. The Chinese are going in and doing the projects that most of the Western companies won't do. Without the Chinese doing a lot of infrastructure projects that are currently going on in Africa, it won't be done. Who else is going to loan the money to actually do it? Once the roads are in place, then it opens up the countries to all sorts of investment opportunities. I would view the Chinese as a great advantage in Africa, because they are doing that work which is required to put the infrastructure and the telecommunications in place. All that stuff is done by Chinese companies under Chinese government financing. It's proper investment, you know what I mean?*

Their successes notwithstanding, Chinese companies are encountering pressure to change in order to remain successful. Among the

---

* On this point, Aidan's head of external affairs, Rosalind Kainyah, really brings the point home. "What the Europeans and Americans could use," she said, "is fewer conferences on China and Africa, and more investment in Africa."

most widely heard pressures on Chinese companies is to manufacture more in Africa.

That exhortation is reasonable, and also applicable to Western companies. It is not clear that China is actually behind in this area. At the national level, there is little to complain about. What data there are indicate that China together with other emerging partners, notably India, Korea, Brazil, and Turkey, are actually more invested in African manufacturing than are Africa's more traditional partners in Europe and North America.[7]

Among individual companies, there may be a greater distinction. Nearly every U.S. or European company with significant African growth targets has a program to develop local suppliers. Most Chinese companies either don't have such programs or don't discuss them publicly, and pressure is rising on them to change. A notable exception may be the telecommunications provider Huawei, which reports having one thousand African subcontractors with whom it spends in excess of $480 million annually.[8] Those are figures comparable with or superior to the largest Western investors in Africa. However, neither Huawei nor most Western companies have their local supplier or local content figures audited. Local content regulations are growing in Africa, and it is reasonable to expect data on local supplier usage and development will become more robust in the years ahead.

The exhortation to Chinese companies to manufacture more locally, while recognizing they have made some inroads already, is reflected in a thought Aidan Heavey shared on the topic:

> I would say in terms of stimulating local economy, this is where the Chinese have to be careful because it's where they are racing to shoot themselves in the foot. As they make investments in these countries, they should not take away the low-barrier entry

manufacturing sectors that allow countries to benefit their own local home markets. I think about cotton producers selling cotton to the Chinese and those cotton producers are buying Chinese shirts. There is a big risk of losing any kind of goodwill. I think there is an opportunity to do that differently. There's no shortage of Chinese that set up looms and clothing manufacturers in Africa. The Chinese have been involved in Africa for quite a while. Some of their entry into Africa wasn't right because they used a lot of Chinese labor and Chinese food was shipped in. It was viewed very badly locally. I think the Chinese have learned very, very quickly, and I think they now are a good partner in Africa.

An even greater focus than the procurement of Chinese supplies is Chinese companies' use of Chinese labor, particularly on major construction sites. Chinese labor in Africa has been a source of friction in many countries where Chinese companies are active. Estimates vary, but Chinese press agency Xinhua estimates that there are more than eight hundred thousand Chinese workers in Africa.[9] Chinese construction practices will matter more to the business community as the private sector grows and engages in a larger portion of building in Africa. That is happening all across the continent. Tony Elumelu's Transcorp is currently building three hotels in Nigeria, and recently won its bid to privatize a large Nigerian power plant. Both projects require major construction efforts. Tony is adamant that "The projects will go to whoever can do the best job and has the right price and timing, whether Chinese, African, Arab, or whatever." I asked him for his view on use of Chinese labor by Chinese companies. "Using only Chinese labor does not build the social wealth of the country," he said, "so it's not really consistent with my view of what works for Africa. If African workers need to be trained, we will want to see that training. If the issue is cultural, as is sometimes the case, then we believe you can help adjust the culture of those workers so that they are suitable for the job. That is how the future needs to be."

Finally, Chinese companies are under increasing pressure to be more transparent in their dealings with government. ECP's Tom Gibian has observed Africa and Asia long enough to take a historical perspective on China's evolution with regard to transparency:

Let's say for a moment that there is a whiff of corruption or outright corruption among Chinese companies. If you look at American, or Italian, or French companies that are involved in Africa, it's difficult to argue that every model that was used by European companies to make investments in Africa has been above reproach and above criticism. The smart ones have figured out it's not worth it, but as a group, it took time. So why can't the Chinese likewise learn to invest in a way that's above reproach and above criticism? They'll figure it out, and if they make mistakes and somebody gets mad at them, that's how you learn from your mistakes. It seemed to me that it's better for China to show up and be part of what's going on, as imperfect as they may be, and that creating more opportunities is better than less opportunities.

The process may indeed proceed as Tom suggests, with a lot of learning by osmosis. I have worked on two mega-projects in which Chinese were partners with a Western company, one in Africa and one in Asia. In both cases, my observation was that the Chinese partner (in both cases a minority partner) was prepared to adhere to the governance and transparency practices of the Western partner. Moreover, the Chinese managers seconded to the project were clearly in "observation" mode, learning if not yet adopting.

That process of learning and osmosis may be compelled to

accelerate by demands from Africa, including from Africa's business leaders. Mo Ibrahim is not sanguine about Chinese participation in corruption or a slow walk toward a cleaner path. He calls on them to meet the same standards his foundation sets for African governments: "China needs to start from where the West is currently," in regard to transparency, "not from where the West started. We do not want to go back."

CHAPTER 8

What About the United States?

I think of Americans when they went to the West. Why did they
go? Because it was empty.

Dr. Chris Kirubi, Chairman, International House Limited

Being in Africa doesn't just make us better in Africa. It makes us
better everywhere.

Jeff Immelt, Chairman and CEO, General Electric

African CEOs talk about the United States often, and at surprising depth. U.S. institutions, economic model, and culture are more
top of mind than our proximity, trade, and investment might suggest. African bilateral trade with the U.S. in 2010 was 12 percent of
Africa's total, less than its trade with Europe or China.[1] The stock
of FDI from the U.S. into Africa is second to France's, but is overwhelmingly concentrated behind the fence-lines of natural resource
operations.[2]

Despite a relatively low level of engagement, Africans have an
overwhelmingly favorable impression of the United States. "The
U.S. is popular for a lot of Africans," Nigerian Tony Elumelu said.
"Even in the very Muslim parts of our country, you will see kids on
the street with an Obama T-Shirt. I myself stayed up watching each

159

of your presidential debates and your election. I am always surprised the U.S. does not do more with this." The most recent Pew Global Opinion survey supports Tony's assertion. In his native Nigeria, U.S. favorability is 81 percent. For comparison, the most recent European favorability rating in Nigeria is 67 percent.[3]

African business leaders are familiar with U.S. history, or more precisely the ideals that emerge from that history. The anticolonial origins of the United States, the pioneering of the West, and the rise of our continental economy are elements of America's past that African business leaders know and that resonate for them. Each of these eras has a darker side, with large numbers excluded or pushed aside. Nonetheless, the ideals that emerge from them of entrepreneurialism, daring, and the "taming" of a continent are new and powerful in Africa.

Vimal Shah sees Africa today as a continental economy in the making, a challenge U.S. companies have mastered before. Speaking of the railroads and telegraph magnates that linked the U.S. economy, he said, "Yes, that's what's needed. Now if you have that, what they had, if you have that adventurous spirit—Africa is waiting."

Chris Kirubi sees clearly the historic link with the American West. "I think of Americans when they went to the West. Why did they go? Because it was empty. So why don't they use the same principles and come to Africa? You can go and build a skyscraper where one's already built. You can build on top of it another one, but why don't you come here and say, 'There are no first-class hotels. There are no motels on the roadside between Nairobi and Mombasa. We're going to build the motels. There are no fast-moving railroads. Why don't we go to Africa and build them from south to north?'"

Bharat Thakrar is keenly aware of the entrepreneurialism at the roots of American capitalism, and relates it to his parable for engaging Africa. "Crossing the Mara is second nature to you," he said. "Just look at when the immigrants settled in the U.S. or when they migrated West. It was not easy but the guys with the nerve went and did it. They went, they settled, and they succeeded."

Some U.S. companies are advancing already. Coca-Cola, Cummins, and GE are among them. The Corporate Council on Africa has 149 U.S. corporate members, each expanding its business in Africa.

A few U.S. companies are engaged in the most important advances on the continent. The Main One subsea high-bandwidth cable was built and brought onshore by U.S. engineering firm SubCom, a division of Tyco Electronics. Main One CEO Funke Opeke works with them still, and sees more opportunity for others:

Our cable was built by an American company and we still have a great relationship with SubCom. We did a $180 million contract with them to get the cable built and they've successfully delivered and continue to support it. Now, perhaps they were unique in that sense, because they build cables around the world and they were open to working with us and just making it happen; they built the SEACOM system* as well. I wish some of the other American companies that we want to do business with, software and telecommunications companies, were half as interested in doing business with us, because we'd be able to achieve a lot more with them.

Another American business that has seen this opportunity and acted on it is Indiana-based Cummins, Inc. Tim Solso spent his entire adult life in that company, from graduation at DePauw until his retirement in 2011 (Tim continues to be active in American industry as one of the new slate of board directors leading General Motors). The story of Tim's, and eventually Cummins's, decision to invest in

---

* SEACOM is a subsea high-bandwidth cable serving East Africa, as Main One serves West Africa.

Africa speaks to what U.S. companies can do in Africa. It includes a few wrong steps along the way, and many of the right ones.

As a young man, Tim's impression of Africa was similar to that of many Americans:

> When I thought of Africa, I really was thinking about the wild game and the animals and habitat and that type of thing. I also thought it was a place with a lot of conflict, civil wars, the residue of colonialism, and extreme poverty. And then there was the whole South African apartheid: the riots and the killing of people, forced segregation, and that type of thing. So it was an exotic place in terms of the wildlife but a continent that suffered a great deal. The biggest misconception I probably had was that I thought of Africa as one entity as opposed to fifty-four or fifty-five countries that are very, very diverse.

Tim's first professional engagement with Africa was in 1981 as the managing director of Cummins subsidiary Holset Engineering. Tim was asked to assess an opportunity to invest in apartheid-era South Africa. He described both a trip and a conclusion that might seem unusual for a young Midwestern executive with a promising career and a lot on the line:

> Because of the boycotts, the South African government couldn't get diesel engines for military equipment, so they put out a request for bids to engine manufacturers to manufacture in South Africa. I was asked to make a recommendation to our leaders on the opportunity in front of us. The subsidiary I was leading made turbochargers for Cummins and others, and we already had distribution there. I took a trip to South Africa to meet with the distributors, but went on my own unaccompanied. While there, I met government officials, members of civil

society, Afrikaans, English, and people they were then calling colored. While I was in Stellenbosch, I also made the decision to meet in private with some people who were protesters or rebels, and were wanted by the government.

The way I saw our challenge, the most important assessment I had to make was whether we, as one manufacturer in South Africa, could pay good wages and make a difference from within, or was apartheid so bad that you needed to get out and stay out until they fix their problem. Before I made a recommendation to Cummins, I wanted a personal education on what the issues were, and to talk to as many different people with different perspectives as I could get. Ultimately, my view was that if you could put the right terms in the bid, for example, pay equal wages and have no segregation in our workplace, that it was worth trying to do.

Despite the finding, Cummins ultimately did not bid on the opportunity and withdrew from South Africa until apartheid ended. But Tim's emphasis on both commercial opportunity and social context, and his insistence on meeting broadly, would also characterize his return to Africa some twenty-five years later as CEO, when he elected to explore Africa as a whole and as a far larger and more strategic opportunity for the company.

Successful business leaders in Africa see America's opportunity in Africa as very much still in front of it. "America has not missed an opportunity," said James Mwangi of Equity Bank. "It is availing itself now. Africa is just coming to the point that U.S. technology and capital is going to be most useful."

The data support that case across multiple sectors. With the exception of South Africa, Africa is only beginning its journey from primary commodity production to modern manufacturing. Figure 8–1 shows the manufacturing value addition—a measure

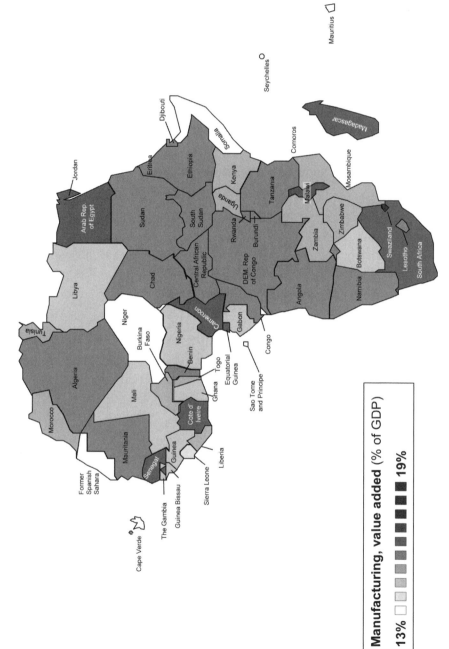

Figure 8–1: Manufacturing value addition in Africa as % of GDP

of manufacturing density—in the major economies of Africa. The relatively low percentages, combined with the young demographic described in chapter 3, speak to the opportunities for the United States to engage with Africa in its early stage of manufacturing, including agroprocessing. Beyond manufacturing, U.S. providers of health and education, two social services that are quickly privatizing, are among the most respected in Africa. And the consumer goods and retail sectors so well documented by the McKinsey Consumer Insight Center are both sectors in which U.S. firms are globally competitive.

In Jeff Immelt's experience at GE, it is precisely in production and related activities that the opportunities in fast-growth markets lie, rather than exports alone.

You are not going to win in a place if you treat it like a sales outpost. It doesn't work anywhere. If you want to be a good global company you have to know how to make money in a country and for a country. If you don't understand that, you're never going to win.

Can we build a factory? Can we do product development? What is the best thing U.S. companies do outside the U.S.? We train people. We have the best industrial training in the world. Turns out, that's kind of important. That actually makes you welcome. You have got to have roots and make some substantial investments that embed you. You have to be part of the fabric of the country.

The Challenges to U.S. Business

Why aren't more U.S. companies succeeding in Africa as Coca-Cola, GE, and Cummins are? African CEOs point to three characteristics of their engagement with U.S. firms that often inhibit the companies' ability to succeed in Africa. While that critique can be painful to absorb, it comes from executives who are admirers of and advocates for the United States. And, as proven by the U.S. executives who are succeeding, there are U.S. companies overcoming these traits, each of which can be remedied.

What Holds Us Back: Hesitance

With remarkable consistency, successful African executives say U.S. corporate engagement in Africa is characterized by more hesitance and a lower tolerance for uncertainty than that of their global competitors.

Vimal Shah feels the opportunities for U.S. firms are vast, but observes resistance on the part of some U.S. firms to undertake the challenges and uncertainty of Africa:

> The U.S. has definitely not missed its opportunity yet. But I don't see the Americans displaying the aptitude or the attitude to win in Africa. The biggest challenge I find is that Americans are in their comfort zone. They are comfortable where they are, and ask why bother with all of this sort of thing in Africa? You don't seem to have many more adventurers, the ones going to explore things. My sense is that today's U.S.-based global firms want everything given. "Until the roads are right, until the power is done, until the political systems are right, we cannot come." I find they are waiting for perfection.

In Vimal's view, one driver of American reticence in Africa is the way in which managerial decision making and authority are organized among some U.S. companies:

> I used to be the chairman of the Kenyan Association of Manufacturers and we had American companies who were already

operating here. A U.S. consumer goods company was one of them. When we turned to doing some joint planning, one of the fellows from their Africa team said, "If we were working for you we could authorize these things. As it is, we report to Egypt. Egypt reports to Switzerland. Switzerland reports to the U.S." That company is one size fits all.

There is a U.S.-based global bank that has been in Africa for decades. It has all it takes to succeed. They've got the technology, they've got fantastic assets here, and a big network, but because they are losing out on opportunities. They are giving it away because the guys that make the decisions are sitting in the U.S. and may have never been to Africa. They will read the papers and say, "What is the GDP growth of each country?" and look at the net growth. Then they will look at the small economies, and tick them off, "Not interested, not interested." So they will have a presence, but not do much. There is no aggressive growth strategy. As a contrast, take an Equity Bank and James Mwangi. He started from zero and today he has built up a fantastic model and a new niche. The U.S. bank looked at the same customers and said, "No, no—that's not my market. We're only working for multinationals, for the big boys."

Chris Kirubi diagnosed what nearly a dozen African CEOs subsequently pointed out. He stated his perspective even as pictures of the American president and U.S. Constitution rolled by on his screensaver. "Americans have to have a positive mind," he said. "You have to see opportunity and be committed. You have to act but you do not. Of course, there are many reasons why not to succeed and why not to act."

Like Chris, Tony Elumelu could not be a bigger fan of the United States. He conducted his mid-career training in the U.S., opened United Bank of Africa's first office in the U.S., and sits on an advisory panel to the U.S. government on African entrepreneurship. "I respect the United States tremendously," he said, "but with all due respect to my American friends, many Americans do not travel, and so the opportunities to see beyond their borders are very limited."

By contrast, Cummins's Tim Solso traveled. He traveled when assessing South Africa for Cummins as a young man in 1981. Twenty-five years later as CEO, he was keen to find Cummins's next big growth opportunity and traveled again…a lot. Tim described where, and why.

Due to some very far-sighted decisions by CEOs before me, we were already well established in India, China, and Brazil. Those decisions were making me and the company look great, and I had a sense that Africa could be the place that I could do the same for the company ten years from now. So, I went to look. I went to South Africa, Zimbabwe, Zambia, Tanzania, Kenya, Egypt, Morocco, Senegal, Ghana, Nigeria, and Angola. One trip led to another because I didn't want to make assumptions that could be desperately wrong and in order to do that, I think you needed to visit all five regions.

If you're sitting in Columbus, Indiana, and never visit Africa you'll never win there. Before we launched our current joint venture in Nigeria, I remember thinking that Nigeria was a corrupt and dangerous place and not to be dealt with. Well, if you go into Nigeria, there are fifty million people that rely on standby generators to get their electricity. It's a huge, huge market. We needed to think about how we operate safely, how we put in ethical safeguards, so we can tap it. You have to flip the equation. How do we work there?

What Holds Us Back: Paternalism

Once U.S. companies are on the ground, African business leaders report their opportunities can be undermined by a posture of paternalism. If Chinese business leaders succeed in Africa in part because they confer dignity and equality in their relations, American businesses are sometimes hurting themselves with the opposite. "The U.S. relationship is influenced by the past," said James Mwangi. "You treat Africa the same way you did in the '60s and '50s, but we have changed." Ironically, the change to which James refers comes *from* America:

> You have provided a huge opportunity for Africans to get the best education, as good as the best that is being offered to American children. The young African executive, to a great extent, has been educated in American universities. His culture and socialization is very different from that of the people you dealt with in the '50s. Yet you want to treat that Harvard graduate managing an African operation the way you treated his father, who was educated in a mission school in Kenya, under the lien of colonialism. Africa is changing faster than America is willing to change your practice and style of engagement.

James has seen the adverse effect on U.S. businesses in his own sector. Speaking of information technology systems in the banking sector, James said, "The American technology is of superior quality, much better than the technology from the East. But the pride and dignity of our people is priceless. People are willing to pay the price of lower quality if their dignity, respect, and esteem are upheld."

The perception of American businesses as sometimes being paternalistic is not entirely their own doing. It is due in part to a lingering perception of U.S. public policy and diplomacy. Fairly or otherwise, many successful African businessmen perceive arrogance in some of the ways our government engages Africa. "When the Americans or American-controlled institutions come," said James Mwangi, "they interact with our African governments in this way that is quite weird. They do not say, 'What do you need?' as the Chinese do. They say, 'This is what you need.'"

Tony Elumelu feels that the tone of U.S. engagement can sometimes be demeaning in a way that has adverse effects on U.S. business interests. "When American presidents go to China, they talk about trade," he said. "When they come to Africa, they lecture us. They need to engage better, including with the African private sector."

James I. Mwangi described a manifestation of this phenomenon in the way the United States treats Africans after they finish university in the U.S. "The U.S. has a resource in Africans graduating from top American schools," he said. "If the U.S. were more open to them staying and working in the U.S. for a few years, you would get several years of good utility from them. It would also cement a really favorable impression of the U.S. with many of the people who will be leading Africa in the future. That would serve the U.S. better than frog-marching these graduates directly to the airport upon getting their diploma, which essentially is what has been happening ever since 9/11."

To be fair, the Obama administration has sought to shift the official dialogue to a more commercial footing. On June 14, 2012, the White House announced a new *U.S. Strategy Toward Sub-Saharan Africa*. The new strategy particularly emphasized spurring economic growth, trade, and investment. Secretary of State Hillary Clinton spent two weeks visiting nine countries across Africa to promote that agenda of increased U.S. economic engagement with the continent, accompanied by executives of U.S. companies.[4] As of this writing, far-reaching immigration reform is moving through the U.S. Senate.

If passed, it is likely to dramatically enhance the opportunities of highly trained Africans to work in the U.S.

Further, the U.S. development program includes several high-profile agencies whose mandate is precisely the facilitation of trade and investment, not charity. The U.S. Overseas Private Investment Corporation, the U.S. Exim Bank, and the Millennium Challenge Corporation each represents a significant apparatus of U.S. policy that promotes trade, investment, and a relationship of equals.

Despite these measures, many of the successful African executives I know think of U.S. government engagement in Africa as consisting of only one tool: charitable aid. I once accompanied ten African CEOs in a meeting with the Millennium Challenge Corporation (MCC). Founded by George W. Bush, the MCC is a great organization that finances development specified by the recipient country, including representatives of the corporate sector in that country. Shortly after the meeting started, the senior executive on the MCC side could sense there was some confusion in the room. To his great credit, he paused the meeting. "May I ask how many of you gentlemen have worked with the MCC?," he inquired. None of the CEOs raised their hands. "May I ask how many of you had heard of the MCC before this meeting was scheduled?" None raised his hand. "Thank you," he said. "This is a very enlightening moment for me and for my staff."

Though few Africans mention it, I believe one reason this perception of paternalism persists is the close association of the United States with Europe. In describing "U.S." attitudes, several African CEOs described actions and policies actually promulgated by European countries. More than one CEO referred to an incident in which a diplomat is purported to have said the corruption of senior figures in the Kenyan government was tantamount to "vomiting all over the shoes" of Western countries. The diplomat in question was in fact British, but the story is nonetheless told and retold to reflect the arrogance of all Western countries, including the U.S. In this regard, the broad brush with which we once painted Africa is wielded as easily on us.

The benefits of U.S.–European coordination in development and in Africa policy are real and overwhelming. However, it is also true that the European relationship with Africa has roots in a colonial past. For many Africans (and Europeans), that past is very much alive today. The U.S. can lead its allies in establishing a new paradigm rooted in a relationship of equals. Policy makers would be well served to vet every policy and every communication with an eye toward reinforcing that new paradigm.

American businesses can also lead in setting the tone of interaction with Africa. When Tim Solso traveled to assess the opportunities across Africa, he went on a listening tour, mostly listening to Africans. And he had the humility to see where Cummins needed to change. "Being around African CEOs and listening to them talk about what their challenges are and what successful strategies work in Africa was incredibly helpful," Tim said. "I had a previously scheduled trip to South Africa, Zambia, and Zimbabwe, where we had distribution, and I could see how bad Cummins was doing and that the model, if you could call it that, was exactly what the African CEOs said would not work." Tim is frank in his assessment of his company's operation:

Basically, the old Cummins has a distribution system that was owned by a European trading company run by expatriates. Following my meetings with African CEOs, when I went I could see we were suffering from this colonial leftover or residue. The people that we had representing Cummins were expatriates, not Africans, and many were at the end of their careers. They were just going through the motions. We had centralized decision making, so decisions about Africa were made in Columbus, Indiana. I also saw that each country was operating on its

own, whereas the African CEOs I know had told me they organized by trading regions. And then, finally, I saw we were doing
no training at all on service.

Based mostly on what I learned from the Africans, we put
in place two pillars of our strategy. We established five regional
operations based on trading blocks. Within each region, we
could see what our mix of business was going to be, and our
priority countries. We also rethought what would be decided
in corporate headquarters and what would be done in the field,
with the vast majority of decision-making capability moved to
the field. We replaced a lot of the European expatriates so that
those decisions would be made by Africans, mostly in their own
countries.

We also made a massive commitment of resources in finding
people and training them to service our equipment. We realized that if we could take care of African customers quickly, it
would be a huge differentiator. I was in Lagos, Nigeria, and we
had lunch with a very small customer there, a plastic extrusion
plant that manufactures lawn furniture. I was seated next to a
woman who was the plant manager. She operated the factory
365 days a year, twenty-four hours a day, and about 90 percent
of her power came from generator sets. At the start of lunch,
she would not buy a Cummins generator. By the end, she said,
"If you could have a technician that knows what they're doing
with the right parts at my factory to fix the gen set in two hours,
I'll buy your sets, no one else's, and I'll pay you whatever you
want." That stuck with me. In many of the markets in Africa,
service capability is nonexistent. If you can deliver service, you
massively differentiate your products and your company.

Building up a service capability across an entire continent takes
time, and Cummins committed to the long term. "Each of our

businesses committed $15 million over five years, for a total of $75 million with no expectation of return over that time," Tim said. "A large portion of that investment is going into training that local workforce." It is that commitment of time that may most distinguish success in Africa from failure.

What Holds Us Back: Haste

Business leaders succeeding in frontier markets constantly identify such long-term thinking as essential to success. U.S. companies do not always exhibit it. Main One CEO Funke Opeke fears U.S. companies will fail to capture the market opportunity in Africa precisely because it is nascent today, and credits Cummins for avoiding that trap:

> If you just looked at what the market opportunity is today, a U.S. company might find it a very small market and so not pay attention or invest. But then the opportunity for later growth—10 percent, 15 percent, 20 percent of their business in the years to come—will be missed. In my sector, I think of opportunities like cloud computing or building data centers. ICT penetration and Internet utilization are so low in Africa today, many U.S. companies would dismiss it. But it's clearly going to grow exponentially. This is the ideal time for companies with that capability to say, "I'm going to build a data center and help drive these services, so that as the sector grows, I'm the dominant player in that market." I think there are some American companies that are doing that right, in different sectors. Cummins, in particular, is one company that I see developing such an African strategy, and I see them implementing and growing along that path in countries including Nigeria.

Neville Isdell of Coca-Cola is unambiguous that this is what he thinks prevents U.S. companies from succeeding in Africa most of all:

Number one is that it's a slow build. U.S. companies, in general, don't have the long-term view that they need to have. They need to plant seeds for the future. The Germans do it differently. They have a very long-term view and, obviously, some of the Asians are doing exactly the same thing. It's not just that they have a different business culture, but also the demands on the business are different; the demands on the CEO for quarterly earnings, etcetera, don't allow that to happen to the same degree in U.S. companies. If a U.S. CEO says he or she's building something for twenty-five years from now, an investor is likely to say, "Oh, come on. I'm not going to invest in you. You're wasting my money."

I asked Neville how he convinced a board and shareholders to take those long bets at Coca-Cola. His answer was wry but also telling. "Well, having shareholders like Warren Buffet helps," he said. "Warren looks for long-term value, so he shared this view. But also as a company we have seen this everywhere, so we expect it. Young markets need a long investment horizon."

In the famously short-term U.S. investment culture, business leaders will need a shared understanding with owners that a viable strategy for success in Africa at scale means a long-term investment. Olam's Sunny Verghese reflected on his own challenges in conveying to some investors the necessity for long-term investment in frontier markets:

We are very long term in our view in terms of these investments, but today, the average time an institutional shareholder stays in a business has come down to between five and six months from eight years or so, which is what it was in the 1980s. As an owner–manager—I see myself first as an owner and then as a CEO—I find it challenging to put myself in the shoes of a temporary, transient, visiting shareholder of my business and still develop long-term strategies. Instead, we have to continuously put ourselves in the shoes of a continuing shareholder and develop the strategy that maximizes their long-term value rather than a short-term payoff. When we launched the current growth strategy, a couple of investors said to me, "I'm not going to be a shareholder in five and seven years' time; I'm sure you're not going to be the CEO in five and seven years' time, so what really motivates you to take such calls and make such decisions?" But these are exactly the decisions you need to be making in these markets.

Cummins likewise benefitted from its past experience developing frontier markets. That history gave the company's investors, board, and management team the confidence to invest in Africa over the long term. Tim Solso describes the company's experience and its effect on their Africa planning:

We went into India in 1962, Brazil in 1972, and China in 1975, and those three markets were a tremendous value to Cummins during the recession of the last part of 2008 to the middle part of 2010. I was able to build on those investments. That's why I was able to say, "Where should we be investing so that ten years from now we're a world leader in that market?"

If you went back and you looked at our history in India, China, and Brazil, the big returns really only came at the beginning of 2003 and 2004. Now, we probably could have done a lot better in terms of how we manage those businesses. Still, they set a realistic expectation for all of us that that these things just don't happen overnight.

Africa is a long-term opportunity, and U.S. companies without appetite for that might indeed defer engagement with Africa. For those with the appetite and resources, operating in Africa also has short-term advantages. Among these is the opportunity to raise the culture of entrepreneurship in the firm and develop a cadre of ambitious leaders to support it. SABMiller experienced this firsthand. Graham Mackay describes it:

We had a relatively large number of competent managers who were keen to spread their wings and run a business with more independence. A good part of our initial commercial success depended on that move into Africa in which our managers gained experience in running a business. It was a salutary experience for many of our people to be put for the first time in a generalist environment where the buck stops at them; they've got to do everything. They have a very broad responsibility for every activity in the business, rather than a highly specialized role. Even if they were in general management before, it was with a great big mother ship all around them. It is very testing, and very good for your career to do it early on at SABMiller. Increasingly, we've seen those African countries as proving grounds for all management.

Jeff Immelt has experienced that executive testing himself over a 31-year career with GE, and considers it a core benefit for managers now working in Africa:

If you ask an American CEO of my generation what the single most interesting and meaningful professional experience is that's changed his life and made him more reflective, more experienced, and more valuable, it would be globalization.

Learning how to go someplace and be a complete nobody is great experience. Having to build from scratch. I've had to work in places where people would say "GE. Is that a division of GM? Do you work for GM?" It made me a better person and a better manager.

A Bigger, Brighter Future

While African business leaders admire the United States, I found some of what they said about U.S. businesses surprising and at odds with what I understand U.S. business to be. Bob Rubin had the same reaction, in particular to what African business had shared about U.S. corporate hesitancy. "I don't agree with that," he said, "not at all. Look at how much of the technological development in the world takes place in this country. It's a goal-oriented, entrepreneurially oriented culture."

That's true of the U.S. technology sector today and has characterized broad swaths of the U.S. economy at different stages of its history. Constant innovation, investment in the face of uncertainty, and vast room for both error and success are features that make the U.S. technology sector a powerhouse today. They also characterize the opportunity in Africa for a broad set of mature industries in the United States.

Mike Rieger is the TE SubCom executive who worked with Funke Opeke to lay the Main One subsea cable. It's one of two major subsea cables SubCom has laid in Africa. The company has its roots in Bell Labs, and was part of the team that laid the first trans-Atlantic phone cables between North America and Europe in the 1950s. "We need to stay at the frontier to win," Mike said. "That has always been our history. First between the U.S. and Europe, then to Japan, Asia, and

Latin America and now Africa. Working with companies like Main One keeps us at that frontier, where we continue to see growth." Most recently, the New Jersey–based SubCom is bidding on subsea cables linking Africa to Brazil, part of a broad "south–south" growth area for the company.

SubCom, like Cummins, is symbolic of the way U.S. companies are evolving and winning in Africa. Though pointed in his counsel to U.S. companies, James Mwangi expressed optimism for prospects in the United States and its relationship to his market. "America is going to be able to reinvent itself," he said. "I'm not sure Europe will be able to. So the question is, what is America's role? What will it reinvent itself as?"

I would describe it not so much as a reinvention as a rediscovery. Africa is a continent where bureaucracy is declining, where optimism in the private sector is rising, and where there is more opportunity than constraint. While the commercial opportunity is quantifiable, the true opportunity for U.S. companies may be in reigniting the dynamism elusive in more mature markets. GE's Jeff Immelt captures that perspective in considering what Africa means to GE, even beyond the income and revenue generated there:

What makes companies like ours competitive is that we have had to go to every corner of the world and sing for our dinner. I find the challenges of Africa to be immensely personally exciting, as I think others in GE do. It makes us humble and challenges the company to transform again. You always need to be throwing the company in front of challenges like this. It makes us faster, it makes us more entrepreneurial. Being in Africa doesn't just make us better in Africa. It makes us better everywhere.

Epilogue

In writing *Success in Africa,* I had no aspiration to save Africa. Africa needs no saving. But in the process, I found that Africa might just help "save" the United States and the role of corporations in national life. Like Adam Smith, I believe in markets serving society. In Africa there are many examples of that happening, and there is space for it to happen more.

Though we often think of it as old, Africa is a new place in almost every way. Its governments are young and its people are young. Its economies are young and growing rapidly. It is time to replace our old image of Africa with this new one.

Africa is a place to be understood in parts and in the whole. Its diversity has at times led to underperformance and even war, but ultimately that diversity is a rich heritage and a source of opportunity. The emerging business leadership in Africa is drawing the continent closer together, displacing local cronyism with genuine competitive strength, and unleashing the continent's potential as a whole. Investors like ECP's Tom Gibian and industrialists like Cummins's Tim Solso have unlocked value in that differentiated whole.

Africa is a place where opportunity doesn't sit alongside need. Opportunity is embedded in universal need. It's fueled by it. Understanding that need, as Equity Bank's James Mwangi has, and meeting it with invention and dignity have proved a profitable path to growth for African and global businesses alike.

That growth requires embracing uncertainty and embedding leadership deep in operations. Like Vimal Shah's Bidco, successful companies that don't find what they need around them are prepared to build it, lead it, or catalyze it. It's a bigger role than companies typically play in a developed economy, as SABMiller has exemplified. The relationship between companies and government (or at least the relationships that work) are of broad-based collaboration and flexibility, though relationships need not be so flexible as to bend core corporate values. Like Africa itself, *Success in Africa* is filled with companies winning with their values reaffirmed.

But the story of Africa is unfinished. Many of the trends described in *Success in Africa* are still underway, some just beginning. Their outcomes are by no means certain.

Africa is becoming Africa, but as that phrase suggests, Africa's integration is in the present tense. The continent's many trade agreements are still materializing, especially in the regulatory details that really build markets. The East African Community has a free trade zone, but there can still be a schoolteacher shortage in Tanzania and a glut in neighboring Kenya, because cross-border licensing is not harmonized. Many travelers still find it easier to travel between African destinations via Paris, London, or Dubai than directly. In the world of powerful blocs that Mo Ibrahim describes in chapter 3, these practicalities will drive the pace of African opportunity.

Governments create more economic space today than in the past, but Africans will expect more of them going forward. James I. Mwangi reflected that "a certain amount of what we've achieved has just been about government getting out of the way." In some areas, like telecoms, many of them have gotten out of the way smartly, creating space and an enabling environment for a competition that serves the population and advances development. In the future, more will be asked of African governments. In particular, the development of physical and social infrastructure on the continent must be guided by government, even if business's role is large and well-played. Kenya's Vision 2030 is a model on which to build.

On a par with infrastructure is stability. As I was in the final weeks of drafting *Success in Africa,* four African countries faced constitutional crises. In Ghana and Kenya, presidential elections were disputed, but peaceably, and in accordance with the law. These are successes, indicia that Africa will manage crises effectively and in a way that fosters growth. In Egypt, however, the president unilaterally assumed power on the path to passing a disputed constitution. In Mali, an insurrection led to military intervention by France, the recently colonial European power. France's intervention may have been warranted, and events there and in Egypt may turn out fine. However, to foster growth, Africa needs to see fewer solutions of that kind, and more like those in Ghana and Kenya.

Finally, there is Africa's youth bulge. Few topics engender as much hopeful and harrowed rhetoric. There is a steady stream of reports from investors extolling its virtues and from development agencies decrying its dangers. Though I'm generally inclined toward the former, the latter are not unsubstantiated. Africa is not Saudi Arabia, and cannot afford to keep masses of young people on the dole. They will work, in one form or another, to be sure. However, to avoid widespread underemployment and disaffection, African economies will need to generate more productive, stable jobs for the 122 million people joining the workforce this decade.[1] Africa may well not follow the path of European, American, or even recent Asian industrialization, but I would look for sectors to emerge that can absorb large numbers of productive youth, including services and a deepened agricultural sector such as Olam's Sunny Verghese envisions in chapter 4.

If past performance is any indication, Africa's accomplishments since the turn of the century offer hope for each of these trajectories. It is an extraordinarily inspiring place to work.

It's inspiring because it's a turnaround, perhaps the greatest of our lifetimes. Consider Rwanda. For many people my age, it is a word synonymous with tragedy. My colleague on this project, Jonathan Kirschner, is fourteen years my junior. He says that when he sees the word Rwanda, it invokes competence and emerging prosperity. What could speak more plainly to the power of renewal, even in the most dire circumstances?

It's inspiring to be on the frontier, where things are being created. You find the most energized people there, and the greatest opportunities. Many in business seek a comfortable zone and commodify. That's not Africa, and not the people who succeed in Africa. They invent. Consider GE, a 120-year-old company with management systems that help make it the fiercest of competitors in mature markets. Yet GE's leadership enters Africa with the intent to compel innovation in their company, and compel change.

Africa is inspiring because it affords businesspeople an extraordinary—perhaps unrivaled—opportunity to achieve great projects that improve people's lives by the millions. Consider Funke Opeke and Main One Cable, bringing the world's information to a Nigerian market of 170 million people, 71 percent of whom have no Internet today.[2] How many lives will be saved, transformed, and invented by the information that will flow in and out of that cable?

I find those supremely exciting enterprises in which to play a part. Should you become a part of it, I would welcome hearing from you. If Africa is a rising continent, it rises on ambitions like these.

ENDNOTES

CHAPTER 1

1. General Electric, *2012 Annual Report*. Fairfield, CT; 3.
2. The Africa Report, *Top 500 Companies in Africa*. February 2012. http://www.theafricareport.com/Top-500-Companies/top-500-companies.html. Accessed December 10, 2012.
3. McKinsey Global Institute, *Lions on the Move: The Progress and Potential of African Economies* (June 2010), 7.
4. Boston Consulting Group, *The African Challengers: Global Competitors Emerge from the Overlooked Continent* (June 2010), 2.

CHAPTER 2

1. *The Economist*, May 13, 2000.
2. *The Economist*, December 3, 2011.
3. "The 20 Most Powerful People in Africa Business," *Forbes*, April 15, 2011, accessed March 23, 2013, http://www.forbes.com/sites/mfonobongnsehe/2011/04/15/the-20-most-powerful-people-in-african-business/7/.
4. Institute for Economics and Peace, *Global Peace Index, 2012* (June 2012), 9.
5. Rafael Grasa and Oscar Mateos, *Conflict, Peace and Security in Africa: An Assessment and New Questions After 50 Years of African Independence*, 9. (ICIP Working Papers 2010/08).
6. The Center for Systemic Peace, *Global Conflict Trends*, last updated October 31, 2012, accessed December 12, 2012, http://www.systemicpeace.org/conflict.htm).
7. "A Glass Half-full," *The Economist*, March 31, 2012.
8. PricewaterhouseCooper, *The Africa Business Agenda* (July 2012), 9. (pwc.com/theagenda)

9. U.S. Census Bureau, International database, accessed December 20, 2012, http://www.census.gov/population/international/data/idb/infor mationGateway.php.

10. John Metzler, *Making Sense of Post-Colonial Africa, 1960–2007*, (African Studies Center, Michigan State University, 2008), 22, http://ebook browse.com/making-sense-of-post-colonial-africa-1960-2008-adapted -from-original-ppt-d185161372) Accessed December 25, 2012.

11. McKinsey Global Institute, *Lions on the Move*, 20.

12. McKinsey Global Institute, *Lions on the Move*, 20.

13. *Africa's Future and the World Bank's Support to It* (The World Bank, March 2011), 3.

14. "Africa's Mobile Phone Industry 'Booming'" *BBC News*, September 11, 2011, accessed December 18, 2012, http://www.bbc.co.uk/news/world -africa-15659983.

15. UN Commission on Trade & Development, *Mobile Banking: UNCTAD Report, Africa Research Bulletin: Economic, Financial and Technical Series*, 48: 19345A–19346B. doi: 10.1111/j.1467-6346.2011.04259.x. 2012.

16. Mark Mobius, "Africa: Investing in the Cradle of Civilization: Part 2," *Investment Adventures in Emerging Markets*, Franklin Templeton Investments, May 9, 2012, accessed December 28, 2012, http://mobius .blog.franklintempleton.com/2012/05/09/africa-investing-in-the -cradle-of-civilization-part-2/.

17. SABMiller, Annual Report, 2012, accessed December 28, 2012, http:// www.sabmiller.com/files/reports/ar2012/2012_annual_report.pdf.

CHAPTER 3

1. A.A. Taylor, *Sam Jonah and the Remaking of Ashanti* (Johannesburg: Pan MacMillan, 2006), 1–46.

2. Private Equity Africa.com, accessed March 28, 2013, http://www.private equityafrica.com/analysis/africa-2011-pe-deals-close-at-3bn/

3. Peter Wonacott, "An Entrepreneur Weathers a Tumultuous Arab Spring," *The Wall Street Journal*, July 17, 2012.

4. "Cevital Group to Boost Rwanda Agriculture Sector," *The Rwanda Focus*, December 12, 2011.

5. Joe Bavier, "Algeria's Cevital Targets Ivory Coast Expansion," Reuters, June 8, 2012, accessed March 25, 2013, http://www.reuters.com/article/ 2012/06/08/ivorycoast-agriculture-cevital-idAFL5E8H88WN20120608.

6. Ernst & Young, "Growing Beyond," 31.

Endnotes

CHAPTER 4

1. *The Rise of the African Consumer* (McKinsey: Africa Consumer Insights Center, October 2012), 1.
2. Kristina Flodman Becker, "The Informal Economy," *SIDA Fact Finding Study*, March 2004.
3. Friedrich Schneider, *Size and Measurement of the Informal Economy in 110 Countries Around the World*, World Bank Working Paper, (July 2002), 6.
4. Miles Morland, "Notes from Africa 2," (June 2011), 11.
5. Equity Bank Investor Briefing, September 30, 2012, 35.
6. Roland Berger, "Profits through Progress: How Investors Can Help Low Income Countries Building Infrastructure Projects Vital for Growth While Reaping Returns," June 2012, 3.
7. "Cellulant Wins Sh745m Nigeria Subsidy Contract," *Daily Nation*, Nairobi, April 11, 2012.
8. "The African Business" (PricewaterhouseCoopers, July 2011).

CHAPTER 6

1. "The Africa Business Agenda" (PricewaterhouseCoopers, July 2011), 35.
2. "GDP in Current U.S. Dollars—Not Adjusted for Inflation," World Bank national accounts data, World Bank, last updated October 31, 2012, accessed January 5, 2013, http://databank.worldbank.org/data/views/reports/tableview.aspx?isshared=true&ispopular=series&pid=2#.
3. Mo Ibrahim, "Celtel's Founder on Building a Business on the World's Poorest Continent," *Harvard Business Review* (September 26, 2012). Used with permission.

CHAPTER 7

1. scholar.google.com, search conducted January 16, 2013.
2. Nicholas Kristof, "Africa on the Rise," *The New York Times,* June 30, 2012.
3. Vivien Foster, William Butterfield, Chuan Chen, and Nataliya Pushak, *Building Bridges: China's Growing Role as Infrastructure Financier for Sub-Saharan Africa*, World Bank, https://openknowledge.worldbank.org/handle/10986/2614, https://openknowledge.worldbank.org/handle/10986/2614, 16; Richard Schiere and Alex Rugamba, *Chinese Infrastructure Investments and African Integration*, Working Paper Series, AfDB, No. 127, May, 2011, 13.
4. *China–Africa Trade and Economic Relationship Annual Report 2010*, Forum on China Africa Cooperation (FOCAC) June 22, 2011, 2;

Endnotes

Mary-Françoise Renard, *China's Trade and FDI in Africa*, Working Paper Series, AfDB, No. 126, May, 2011, 12–18; "Policy Brief: Chinese Trade and Investment Activities in Africa," *The African Development Bank Group Chief Economist Complex*, Volume 1, Issue 4, July 29, 2010, 2–3; and Peter Wonacott, "In Africa, U.S. Watches China's Rise, *The Wall Street Journal*, September 2, 2011.

5. *Africa Macro—Insight & Strategy, EM10 and Africa: China–Africa Ties Deepen, but on Whose Terms?*, Standard Bank, November 29, 2012, 1.
6. Deborah Brautigam, "China and Oil-Backed Loans in Angola: The Real Story," *China in Africa: The Real Story*, October 17, 2011, accessed January 8, 2013, http://www.chinaafricarealstory.com/2011/10/china-and -oil-backed-loans-in-angola.html.
7. "Africa and Its Emerging Partners," *African Economic Outlook*, 2011, accessed January 9, 2013, http://www.africaneconomicoutlook.org/en/ in-depth/emerging-partners/.
8. *Huawei Africa Fact Sheet*, accessed January 9, 2013, http://www.hua wei.com/ucmf/groups/public/documents/webasset/hw_090307.pdf .
9. Ben Ochieng and Chrispinus Omar, "Co-op with China Boosts African Infrastructure," *China Daily*, October 4, 2012.

CHAPTER 8

1. "International Trade Statistics 2012," World Trade Organization, 2012, accessed January 10, 2013, http://www.wto.org/english/res_e/statis_e/ its2012_e/its2012_e.pdf.
2. Vivian C. Jones and Brock R. Williams, "U.S. Trade and Investment Relations with Sub-Saharan Africa and the African Growth and Opportunity Act," *Congressional Research Service*, November 14, 2012: p. 13.
3. "Opinion of the United States," *Global Attitudes Project*, Pew Research, 2012, accessed January 10, 2013, http://www.pewglobal.org/database/ ?indicator=1.
4. Neanda Salvaterra, "U.S. Aims to Lift Investment in Africa," *The Wall Street Journal*, August 6, 2012.

EPILOGUE

1. David Fine et al, "Africa at Work: Job Creation and Inclusive Growth," McKinsey Global Institute, August 2012, 2.
2. "Internet World Statistics," Miniwatts Marketing Group, 2012, accessed March 20, 2013, http://www.internetworldstats.com/africa.htm.

REFERENCES

African Development Bank Group Chief Economist Complex. *Policy Brief: Chinese Trade and Investment Activities in Africa,* Volume 1, Issue 4 (July 29, 2010).

Boston Consulting Group. *The African Challengers: Global Competitors Emerge from the Overlooked Continent,* June 2010.

Central Intelligence Agency, *African Ethnic Groups.* http://en.wikipedia .org/wiki/File:Africa_ethnic_groups_1996.jpg.

Ernst & Young. *Building Bridges: Ernst & Young's 2012 Attractiveness Survey – Africa,* 2012.

Ernst & Young. *Growing Beyond Borders.* Presented at the Africa CEO Forum, November 2012.

Ernst & Young. *Growing Beyond—Africa by the Numbers: Assessing Market Attractiveness in Africa,* 2012.

Flodman Becker, Kristina. *The Informal Economy. SIDA Fact Finding Study,* March 2004.

Forum on China Africa Cooperation (FOCAC). *China–Africa Trade and Economic Relationship Annual Report 2010,* June 22, 2011.

Foster, Vivien Foster, et al. *Building Bridges: China's Growing Role as Infrastructure Financier for Sub-Saharan Africa.* World Bank, 2009. https:// openknowledge.worldbank.org/handle/10986/2614.

Freedom House. *2012 Freedom in the World.* http://www.freedomhouse .org/report/freedom-world/freedom-world-2012.

Grasa, Rafael Grasa, and Oscar Mateos. *Conflict, Peace and Security in Africa: An Assessment and New Questions After 50 Years of African Independence.* ICIP Working Papers, 2010/08.

Huawei Corporation, *Huawei Africa Fact Sheet.* http://www.huawei.com/ ucmf/groups/public/documents/webasset/hw_090307.pdf.

References

Ibrahim, Mo. "Celtel's Founder on Building a Business on the World's Poorest Continent." *Harvard Business Review,* October 2012.

Institute for Economics and Peace. *Global Peace Index, 2012,* June 2012.

Jones, Vivian C. and Brock R. Williams. *U.S. Trade and Investment Relations with Sub-Saharan Africa and the African Growth and Opportunity Act.* Congressional Research Service, November 14, 2012.

Krause, Kai. *The True Size of Africa.* http://statico2.mediaite.com/geeko system/uploads/2010/10/true-size-of-africa.jpg.

McKinsey & Company Africa Consumer Insight Center. *The Rise of the African Consumer,* October 2012.

McKinsey Global Institute. *Africa at Work: Job Creation and Inclusive Growth,* August 2012.

McKinsey Global Institute. *Lions on the Move: The Progress and Potential of African Economies,* June 2010.

Metzler, John. *Making Sense of Post-Colonial Africa, 1960–2007.* African Studies Center, Michigan State University, 2008.

Michigan State University, Africa Studies Center. *African Religions Map.* http://exploringafrica.matrix.msu.edu/images/africa_religions.jpg

Miniwatts Marketing Group. *Internet World Statistics.* http://www.internet worldstats.com.

Morland, Miles. "Notes from Africa 2." London: June 2011.

NordNordWest. *Official Languages in Africa.svg.* http://commons.wikime dia.org/wiki/File:Official_languages_in_Africa.svg.

Pew Charitable Research Trust. Global Attitudes Project, "Opinion of the United States." http://www.pewglobal.org/database/?indicator=1.

PricewaterhouseCoopers. *The Africa Business Agenda,* July 2011.

Renard, Mary-Françoise, *China's Trade and FDI in Africa* Working Paper Series, AfDB, No. 126, May, 2011.

Roland Berger. *Profits through Progress: How Investors Can Help Low Income Countries Building Infrastructure Projects Vital for Growth While Reaping Returns,* June 2012.

SABMiller. *Annual Report, 2012.* http://www.sabmiller.com/files/reports/ar2012/2012_annual_report.pdf.

Schiere, Richard, and Alex Rugamba. *Chinese Infrastructure Investments and African Integration,* Working Paper Series, AfDB, No. 127, May, 2011.

Schneider, Friedrich. *Size and Measurement of the Informal Economy in 110 Countries Around the World,* World Bank Working Paper, July 2002.

Standard Bank. *Africa Macro—Insight & Strategy, EM10 and Africa: China–Africa Ties Deepen, but on Whose Terms?* November 29, 2012.

References

Taylor, A.A. *Sam Jonah and the Remaking of Ashanti* (Johannesburg: Pan MacMillan, 2006).

The Center for Systemic Peace. *Global Conflict Trends.* http://www.systemicpeace.org/conflict.htm.

The Royce Funds. *Africa: Opportunities and Challenges in a Growing Economy.* http://www.roycefunds.com/news/global/2012/0125-africa-opportunities -challenges-growing-economy.asp.

UN Commission on Trade and Development. *Economic Development in Africa Report, 2011: Fostering Industrial Development in Africa in the New Global Environment,* July 2011.

UN Commission on Trade and Development. *Mobile Banking: UNCTAD Report, Africa Research Bulletin: Economic, Financial and Technical Series,* 48: 19345A–19346B. doi: 10.1111/j.1467-6346.2011.04259.x. 2012.

U.S. Census Bureau, International database. http://www.census.gov/ population/international/data/idb/informationGateway.php.

World Bank Group. *National Accounts Data "Manufacturing, Value Added (% of GDP).* http://data.worldbank.org/indicator/NV.IND.MANF.ZS/ countries?display=map.

World Bank. *Africa's Future and the World Bank's Support to It,* March 2011.

World Bank. *National Accounts Data* http://databank.worldbank.org/data/ views/reports/tableview.aspx?isshared=true&ispopular=series& pid=2#.

World Bank. *Doing Business 2013: Smarter Regulations for Small and Medium-Size Enterprises,* 10th edition, Washington, DC.

World Trade Organization. *International Trade Statistics 2012.* http://www .wto.org/english/res_e/statis_e/its2012_e/its2012_e.pdf.

ACKNOWLEDGMENTS

Hopefully, this book says something new, interesting, and human. If it does, that is a credit to the many people who gave of themselves in its execution.

I owe a great debt to the business leaders and others who agreed to be interviewed and quoted; each provided insight I could get nowhere else. Many offered perspectives on their personal journeys without which this would have been a far less illuminating book for author and reader alike. I am grateful in particular to Robert Rubin who graciously agreed to invest his energies time and again, including in the Foreword.

Some of the participants in *Success in Africa* I've known for years, but many came to the project through friends and colleagues. I am grateful to each of them for bringing me into their relationships. Tom Gibian of ECP, Tony Elumelu of Heirs Holdings, Jennifer Potter of the Initiative for Global Development, and Michael Spicer of Business Leadership South Africa deserve particular acknowledgment for this act of faith.

I am deeply grateful to the 150-odd staff and partners of Dalberg Global Development advisors. James I Mwangi, Madji Sock, and Edwin Macharia were particularly helpful in sharing their insights and networks. Paul Callan, Veronica Chau, Sonila Cook, Vicky Hausman, Yana Kakar, and Andrew Stern took on a heavy management burden that I set down in order to write. My numerous junior colleagues and advisees heard and saw less of me in that time, but were stalwart in their support and enthusiasm. I'm honored to be in their company.

I would certainly have stumbled in this endeavor were it not for the support provided by Jonathan Kirschner. Jonathan is a powerful observer of frontier market commerce and sociopolitical trends. He challenged me at many turns to do better and think harder, armed always with a compelling fact base. This book's failings rest with me, but credit for many of its strengths is due Jonathan.

I was strongly supported throughout by the Bibliomotion community, led by Erika Heilman and Jill Friedlander. Cave Henricks Communications supported publicity and Rusty Shelton helped me navigate social media. Jill Schoenhaut ably and affably managed the book's production. My fellow Bibliomotion authors proved a fantastic support and learning network. In particular, Tom Koulopoulos and Asha Dornfest were valued advisors during this project.

Colleagues with a deep understanding of Africa lent their critical and creative minds to the project. I'm grateful to Isobel Coleman and John Campbell of the Council on Foreign Relations, Mahmoud Mamdani of Morgan Stanley, and Paul Collier of Oxford University for their help framing my earliest thinking and allowing me to revisit and update with them. Eric Askanase lent legal counsel and friendship freely. Ray Short, Darren McDermott, Daniel Lederman, and Denis Duffey are friends of decades whose extraordinary professional talents in communications, economic development, and strategy were gracious gifts and a joy to observe.

Thanks justly summit with family. My parents George and Rochel read each chapter with love and discernment and my brother Joshua, an accomplished scholar and author, provided sound counsel on many points. My in-laws Helen and B.B. Bhattacharyya provided a home away from home on many occasions during the writing. Then there are my wife and son, the bedrock of being. They responded to absence, uncertainty, and inconvenience with unwavering love and support. Without them I could not be, and to them this book is dedicated.

INDEX

Index

Chrysler Corporation, 103
civil service, 32, 123–124
CNN, 2
Coca-Cola Company, 11, 161
    long-term commitments by, 175
    tailoring to local culture at,
        109–110
Cold War, 21–22
collaboration, 133–135
Collier, Paul, 12–13
colonialism, 23
    access to government and, 138
    education and, 31, 34
    languages and, 43–44
    U.S. and, 160, 171–172
commitment, long-term, 132–133,
    149–150, 173–178
Common Market for Eastern and
    Southern Africa (COMESA),
    50–52
communications, 34–38
company towns, 88
conflict, 2, 183
    turnaround in, 17, 19, 184
consumer spending, 6, 73–78
Corporate Council on Africa, 161
corporate culture, 112–113
corporate social responsibility, 86–93
corruption, 115–116. *See also*
    transparency
    China and, 144, 145, 156–157
    consistent positions on, 138–141
    decrease in, 17, 19
coups, 24–26
court systems, 127

cultural differences, 57–58
    corporate culture and, 112–113
    tailoring to, 95, 109–113
Cummins, Inc., 161–163
    economies of scale at, 63
    long-term commitments by,
        176–177
    strategy development, 172–174

D
Dalberg Global Development
    Advisors, 5, 65
demand
    in agriculture, 10
    China and, 146–147
    need-based, ability to pay and,
        73–78
    opportunity based on,
        181–182
    projected, 6
demographics, 6, 183
    growth driven by, 38, 40
    violence and, 23–24
deprivation, feelings of, 67–68
Diop, Cheikh Anta, 69
Diop, Magatte, 118–119, 130
diplomacy, 170–171
Doing Business project, 74,
    117–118

E
Ease of Doing Business rankings,
    138
East African Community (EAC),
    51–52, 182

Index

Index

Index

Index

Index